CARAVAGGIO
ART, KNIGHTHOOD, AND MALTA

Albert Clouwet, attrib., *Portrait of Caravaggio*, engraving from G.P. Bellori, *Vite de' pittori*, Rome 1672

CARAVAGGIO
ART, KNIGHTHOOD, AND MALTA

KEITH SCIBERRAS   DAVID M. STONE

midsea BOOKS LTD
for The History of Art Programme
University of Malta
2006

Published by Midsea Books Ltd.
3a Strait Street, Valletta, Malta
Tel: 2149 7046 Fax: 2149 6904
www.midseabooks.com

Produced by Mizzi Design and Graphic Services Ltd.
Printed at Gutenberg Press Ltd, Malta

ISBN: 99932-7-073-3 (Hardbound)
ISBN: 99932-7-071-7 (Paperbound)

Chapters II and III are revised and expanded from Keith Sciberras and David M. Stone,
'Caravaggio in Black and White: Art, Knighthood, and the Order of Malta (1607–1608)',
in *Caravaggio, The Final Years*, ed. N. Spinosa, exh. cat. (London, The National Gallery, 2005;
previously at Naples, Museo di Capodimonte in 2004–2005), Naples, 2005, pp. 61–79.

Cover: Caravaggio, *The Beheading of St John the Baptist*, Valletta, Oratory of San Giovanni Decollato, detail

N.B. Illustrations: paintings are by Caravaggio unless otherwise noted. Dimensions are height
before width.

Photo Credits:All photographs of Malta and works in Maltese collections are by Daniel Cilia.
Biblioteca Marucelliana, Florence; Alberto Bruschi collection, Florence; Soprintendenza Speciale
per il Polo Museale Fiorentino; The National Gallery, London; Patrimonio Nacional, Madrid;
Heritage Malta; Archbishop's Palace, Mdina (Malta); Museo Regionale, Messina; Pinacoteca
di Brera, Milan; Musée des Beaux-Arts, Nancy; Banca Intesa, Naples; Museo di Capodimonte,
Naples; Pio Monte della Misericordia, Naples; Réunion des Musées Nationaux, Paris; Collegio
Wignacourt Museum, Rabat (Malta); Soprintendenza Speciale per il Polo Museale di Roma;
Direzione Generale per il Patrimonio Storico, Artistico ed Etnoantropologico, Rome; Galleria
Regionale, Palazzo Bellomo, Syracuse; the St John's Co-Cathedral Foundation, Valletta; Catholic
University of America, Washington, D.C.

CONTENTS

Preface vii

Chapter I
   Light into Darkness: Caravaggio, 1571–1610 1
   David M. Stone

Chapter II
   Virtuosity honoured, Chivalry disgraced 17
   Keith Sciberras

Plates 41

Chapter III
   'Fra Michelangelo' and the Art of Knighthood 67
   David M. Stone

Chapter IV
   Malta in Late Caravaggio:
   A Chronology for the Final Years 107
   Keith Sciberras

Bibliography 125
Index 135

Fort St Angelo (with post-1608 additions), Vittoriosa

PREFACE

Caravaggio's sojourn on the island of Malta is one of the most dramatic and art-historically significant moments in the Italian painter's life. *Caravaggio: Art, Knighthood, and Malta* is a brief survey of this fascinating period. This book is the result of original research carried out by the two authors in archives, libraries, museums, churches, and private collections throughout Europe and the United States. The fruit of extensive collaboration, the current publication includes a revised and expanded version of the essay, 'Caravaggio in Black and White: Art, Knighthood, and the Order of Malta (1607–1608)', published in the catalogue *Caravaggio, The Final Years* accompanying the extraordinary exhibition held at the Museo di Capodimonte, Naples (*Caravaggio, l'ultimo tempo, 1606–1610*), and the National Gallery, London, in 2004–2005.

Until recently, Caravaggio's Malta period was really only accessible through a dozen or so specialised articles and essays. Indeed, this topic was mostly neglected in scholarship before the mid-1970s. Addressing a variety of issues, Gregori, Calvesi, Azzopardi, Gash, Macioce, and others – including the present authors – have contributed to knowledge about the artist's life and work on the island. A book published by Farrugia Randon in 2004 has distilled much of this information. The present study, while obviously building on earlier research, includes new material and observations, and is the first to integrate the lessons of the Naples–London exhibition into the story of Caravaggio's Maltese experience. Through *Caravaggio, The Final Years,* the Malta period has been launched into the public consciousness as never before. The exciting saga of Caravaggio's life, his powerful network of patrons, and the titanic force of his work have signalled Malta as a crucial phase – indeed, the crucial phase – of his late years.

The first chapter of the book sets the stage for understanding Caravaggio's Maltese art and its critical reception. It outlines his career in a broad art-historical context, highlighting such themes as Caravaggio's technique, formal and iconographic concepts, and stylistic development. The second chapter deals with the documentary evidence for his Maltese sojourn, raising questions about his motives for coming to the island, the identity of his protectors and patrons, the complications of his knighthood, and the nature of the crime that ultimately led to his imprisonment and daring escape to Sicily. Caravaggio painted some of the greatest works of his career for the Knights of Malta. These pictures, including the magnificent *Beheading of Saint John the Baptist,* are the subject of the third chapter. It examines this pivotal moment of Caravaggio's stylistic evolution, when he was painting to please patrons who in many ways held the keys to his liberation from exile. The concluding chapter emerges directly from viewing the exhibition *Caravaggio, The Final Years* in both Naples and London, and discusses highly controversial issues of chronology and attribution that have made headlines in recent years.

We have greatly benefitted from the support and advice of the *Final Years* team of Nicola Spinosa, Dawson Carr, and Keith Christiansen. Each of us has also learned much from conversations with other Caravaggio scholars, including Gioacchino Barbera, Sergio Benedetti, John Gash, Mina Gregori, Helen Langdon, Maurizio Marini, Catherine Puglisi, Ludovica Sebregondi, and John Spike. In Malta, thanks are due to John Azzopardi, former curator, Cathedral Museum, Mdina; Daniela Apap Bologna, former curator, St. John's Co-Cathedral and Museum; Cynthia de Giorgio, curator, St. John's Co-Cathedral and Museum; the St. John's Co-Cathedral Foundation; and other librarians, archivists, and curators. We are also grateful to the Caravaggio Foundation and the co-ordinators of Caravaggio.com. This book would not have been possible without the support of Joseph Mizzi of Midsea Books. It was also much improved by Daniel Cilia's excellent photographs. We thank Mario Buhagiar, Head of History of Art, for the honour of publishing this work under the auspices of the History of Art Programme, University of Malta.

Keith Sciberras   David M. Stone
Valletta, January 2006

Portrait of Alof de Wignacourt and a Page, Paris, Louvre, detail

Aerial view of Valletta

Fig. 1. *Medusa*, Florence, Uffizi

CHAPTER ONE

Light into Darkness:
Caravaggio, 1571-1610

David M. Stone

[Caravaggio]
the great Protopainter,
Marvel of Art,
Wonder of Nature,
Though later a victim of ill fortune.
G.C. Gigli, *La Pittura trionfante*, 1615[1]

When the Knights of Malta invested Caravaggio (frontispiece) with the habit of the Order in July 1608, a year after his arrival on the island, they surely knew not only a lot about his chequered past – brawls, rock-throwing, carrying a sword without a licence, a libel suit, and murder – but also about his magnificent altarpieces in Rome and Naples.[2] They may also have heard tell that, although some of his public religious works had been rejected for their daring iconography and naturalism, the refused paintings had been quickly scooped up by eager connoisseur-collectors.[3] Copied repeatedly,[4] Caravaggio's early allegorical and genre pictures were no less coveted. Poets were inspired by them. In fact, Cavalier Giambattista Marino (1569–1625), the most important Italian literary figure of the age, became Caravaggio's friend and had his portrait made by him.[5] Marino wrote a poem about Caravaggio's terrifying *Medusa* of c. 1598 (fig. 1),[6] a picture some have seen as an oblique self-portrait. Already by 1605 several artists in Rome were beginning to imitate his style, including Guido Reni and Orazio Gentileschi, father of the great female painter Artemisia. Within two decades, Caravaggism would become an international phenomenon, spreading from Velázquez's Spain to Rembrandt's Holland.[7] Protected by cultured members of the

Roman nobility and clergy, and subsequently patronized in Naples by influential families and congregations (significantly, many of these individuals had close ties to the Knights), Caravaggio, by the time of his arrival in Malta, was already one of the most celebrated artists in Italy.[8]

Any assessment of Caravaggio's Malta period (1607–1608) depends on a broad understanding of his artistic formation in Rome and of the development of style and meaning that took place in his art in the immediate aftermath of his terrible crime and flight from the Eternal City at the end of May 1606. Just who was this famous fugitive, who came to Malta to paint for the Grand Master and his fellow Knights?

Michelangelo Merisi da Caravaggio was the most radical painter in Italy in the period following the Council of Trent (1545–1563) and the first phase of the Catholic Reformation it ushered in.[9] Born in 1571, probably in the small town of Caravaggio near Milan,[10] the Lombard painter brought about a reform of his own by openly mocking Roman classical tradition, both in his art and in witty, critical pronouncements that were legendary in his own lifetime. He populated his religious and mythological compositions with figures based on low-class types – 'people in the street' – triumphantly thumbing his nose at the tried-and-true models of ideal beauty that guided the figure style of his late-Mannerist peers. Art theorists such as Monsignor Agucchi and leaders of the Roman art academy such as Federico Zuccaro expounded on the virtues of Michelangelo, Raphael, and antique statuary. They had no more tolerance for Caravaggio's naturalism than nineteenth-century French academic painters and critics had for the Impressionists.[11] Paradoxically, though, Caravaggio often did, in fact, make citations of classical statues and Renaissance paintings, posing his low models after these famous, lofty prototypes.[12] However, the critics either ignored his use of such sources or considered them to be part of an overall campaign of sabotage. According to the writer Félibien, the ultra-classicising painter Poussin (1594–1665) loathed Merisi, remarking that 'Caravaggio had come into the world to destroy painting'. Indeed, this is not an absurd extrapolation of Caravaggio's contempt for tradition, especially if one understands 'painting' to mean the standard theory and practice of Roman art in the last decade of the sixteenth century.

In many of his public religious canvases, Caravaggio not only went out of his way to avoid classicising his figures, whom he often shows with dirty feet and fingernails, dark complexions and rough, weathered skin, he also staged them in realistic, modern settings and clothed them in contemporary costumes. Caravaggio's paintings contain jarring anachronisms that inflamed critics. Even the Carracci, who in the 1580s had revolutionized Italian painting at their Academy in Bologna, had not attacked the artificiality and *all'antica* pretence of the late Maniera so violently.[13]

Symptomatic of this same anti-Mannerist mentality was Caravaggio's elevation of still-life painting, usually considered the lowest category in the hierarchy of genres, to the level of history painting (scenes of religious, historical, or literary subjects). The prime example of this bold challenge to authority is the *Still Life with a Basket of Fruit* of c. 1600–1601 (Ambrosiana, Milan), one of the first independent still life paintings in Italian art. Caravaggio, as recorded by his patron Vincenzo Giustiniani, had the audacity to announce to the Roman art world, that 'it was as difficult for him to make a good painting of flowers as one of figures.'[14] To the establishment in the Eternal City, for whom 'disegno' – drawing the nude human form with the beauty of proportions, clarity of contour, and gracility of line epitomized in Raphael and the antique – was the touchstone of any viable style, such a statement was tantamount to dropping a bomb in the piazza of Roman art theory.

The critics would have their revenge in due course, calling Caravaggio a mere ape of nature, a copyist and conjurer who fooled the eye but failed to elevate art to higher ideals. Emphasizing colour over line (*colore* over *disegno*) was considered by his detractors to be proof positive that he did not know how to draw properly and thus needed to cloak his mistakes in dark shadows. Though Caravaggio must have known how to draw, it seems that he did not develop his ideas through preparatory drawings, preferring instead to sketch directly on the canvas. In the *Vite de' pittori* (1672), Caravaggio's most important biographer, Giovan Pietro Bellori, an ardent classicist who championed the works of Domenichino and Poussin, blamed Caravaggio for leading a whole generation of young artists down the wrong path:

> Nonetheless many artists were taken by his style and gladly embraced it, since without any kind of effort it opened the way to easy copying, imitating common forms lacking beauty. Thus, as Caravaggio suppressed the dignity of art, everybody did as he pleased, and what

followed was contempt for beautiful things, the authority of antiquity and Raphael destroyed. Since it was easy to find models and to paint heads from life, giving up the history painting appropriate for artists, these people made half-figures, which were previously uncommon. Now began the imitation of common and vulgar things, seeking out filth and deformity, as some popular artists do assiduously. So if they have to paint armor, they choose to reproduce the rustiest; if a vase, they would not complete it except to show it broken without a spout. The costumes they paint consist of stockings, breeches, and big caps, and in their figures they pay attention only to wrinkles, defects of the skin and exterior, depicting knotted fingers and limbs disfigured by disease.[15]

This, of course, is a caricature of Caravaggism written by a man worried that the naturalist school Michelangelo Merisi founded would perhaps upstage Roman antique culture.[16] Bellori's general observations, however, are not far from the mark. Indeed, Caravaggio's naturalism was often intended to shock, to bring an audience face to face with the saints and heroes of the past by using the familiar facial types and locations of the present as a bridge. The effect is not unlike a recent film of Shakespeare's *Romeo and Juliet,* set amongst Los Angeles-style street gangs. Caravaggio would have tipped his hat at Jean-Luc Godard, whose film *Je vous salut, Marie* (*Hail Mary*), situates the Holy Family as a lower-class French couple: Mary is a basketball player who pumps gas at her father's service station; Joseph drives a cab. Caravaggio, it seems to me, was reaching for this kind of jarring dislocation, this mix of high and low, long before the concept of the *avant-garde* was invented.

Caravaggio's most important innovation was the creation of a new vocabulary for depicting moments of divine revelation, conversion, or ecstasy by immersing his scenes in a bold *chiaroscuro* (transparent shading) penetrated by a wave of bright light entering the composition from a high, unseen source. Some critics thought Caravaggio painted in his basement; indeed, he may have used a *semi-interrato* (below street-level) studio with high windows in Rome when he first developed his style. The drama of light and dark, always carefully integrated with the poignant gestures, postures, and facial expressions of his actors, gives Caravaggio's images a heightened realism and psychological depth unique to late Renaissance art. It also doubles as a powerful metaphor of divine agency. Caravaggio represents major themes of the Catholic

Reformation – poverty and charity, death and redemption, doubt and faith – in a language that is at once populist, poetic, and spiritual.

Milan 1571–1592

The first child of Fermo Merisi (c. 1538–1577) and his second wife Lucia Aratori (c. 1550 –1590), Caravaggio grew up under the protection of Francesco Sforza, Marchese di Caravaggio (d. 1583), for whom Fermo served as a 'muratore' (a mason).[17] Sforza's widow, Costanza Colonna (d. 1622) provided the artist with introductions and protection throughout his life. She and her son, the knight Fra Fabrizio Sforza Colonna, were close to Grand Master Wignacourt during the period of Caravaggio's visit to Malta.[18]

Caravaggio's earliest period, when he was apprenticed in Milan (c. 1584–1588) to the Bergamasque painter Simone Peterzano, a pupil of Titian, is still a mystery.[19] No securely attributed works made before Caravaggio moved to Rome have been discovered. But judging from the earliest known pictures, it is clear that he had studied numerous Lombard and Venetian masters: Savoldo, Moretto, and Lotto as well as Titian, Giorgione, and Palma Vecchio.[20] Caravaggio's debt to Leonardo, whose naturalism and *sfumato* (modelling through delicate, 'smoky' shading) had transformed Lombard painting in the early sixteenth century, was significant. Bellori states that in Milan Caravaggio earned a living making portraits. The strong visual and psychological bond Caravaggio's compositions create between protagonist and spectator no doubt springs in part from this early interest in portraiture. His practice of painting directly from the model rather than working from drawings (the norm in Rome) may also stem from the same experiences.[21]

Rome 1592–1606

By 1592, or 1593 at the latest, Caravaggio made his way to Rome. He took on menial work until being employed by the Cavalier d'Arpino (Giuseppe Cesari), the most sought-after fresco painter in the city. A practitioner of late Maniera style, d'Arpino seems nonetheless to have appreciated Caravaggio's naturalistic gifts and hired him to

Fig. 2. *Bacchus*, Florence, Uffizi

paint flowers and fruits (whether these were independent still-lifes by Caravaggio or details added to d'Arpino's larger compositions is unknown). Caravaggio's earliest pictures, such as the *Boy with a Basket of Fruit* or the *Bacchino Malato* (Sick Little Bacchus) of c. 1592–1593 (both Galleria Borghese, Rome) are dazzling displays of still life painting. Michelangelo's half-length treatment of eroticized boys in off-the-shoulder, toga-like costumes also attracted attention. Two collectors in particular, Cardinal Francesco Maria del Monte and his friend Marchese Vincenzo Giustiniani, both connoisseurs of music and painting, purchased or commissioned numerous works by Caravaggio in this mode. Del Monte, who hosted the artist in his palace in c. 1596–1600, owned at least ten paintings by him, including the *Concert of Youths* (c. 1595, Metropolitan Museum, New York). Giustiniani owned at least thirteen, including the *Lute Player* (c. 1596,

Fig. 3. *Calling of St Matthew*, Rome, Contarelli Chapel, San Luigi dei Francesi

Hermitage, St Petersburg). The androgynous protagonists and their solicitous gazes have been interpreted in a homoerotic key by several scholars, who note del Monte's reputation as a pederast.[22] Many questions remain, however, about Caravaggio's own sexuality (or bisexuality). There is ample evidence that he had relationships with women. Moreover, it is important to note that with few exceptions, such pictures cease once Caravaggio became known as a serious religious painter. In these early, provocative paintings, Caravaggio has taken a Venetian tradition of half-length, portrait-like images of sexy females posing as mythological goddesses (such as those by Palma Vecchio) and flipped the gender. A good example of this practice is the *Bacchus* of c. 1596 in the Uffizi (fig. 2). The fine line Caravaggio walks here between realism and parody is what makes his art so modern.

Fig. 4. Annibale Carracci, *Assumption of the Virgin,*
oil/panel, Rome, Cerasi Chapel, S.M. del Popolo

In 1599, Caravaggio's career took a major turn when he received
his first commission for a public work. Left incomplete by d'Arpino,
the task of decorating the Contarelli Chapel of the French national
church, San Luigi dei Francesi, gave the young artist his first
opportunity to paint site-specific religious pictures.[23] His paintings
for the side walls (laterals), *The Calling of St Matthew* (fig. 3) and *The
Martyrdom of St Matthew* are exceptional in their clever compositional
structure, skewing perspective axes so as to draw the spectator into
the scene. His bridging of the space of the image and the space of the
spectator – sometimes called 'coextensive' space – would become a
central feature of seventeenth-century painting. His treatment of light
sources is also part of the integration of the work into its environment.
Especially in the case of the *Calling*, we are to understand the light

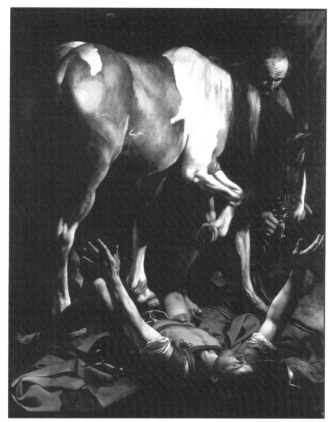

Fig. 5. *Conversion of St Paul,* Rome, Cerasi Chapel, S.M. del Popolo

streaking across the wall behind Christ and Matthew as somehow connected with the natural source of illumination in the chapel – the window directly above the altar. He developed these ideas in his next public commission, in the Cerasi Chapel at Santa Maria del Popolo, where, in competition with Annibale Carracci's robust, classicising altarpiece of the *Assumption of the Virgin* (fig. 4), he painted laterals of the *Crucifixion of St Peter* and the *Conversion of St Paul* (c. 1600–1601). In the latter (fig. 5), Paul, set diagonally to the picture plane, seems nearly to fall out of the frame towards the viewer.

Much has been made of Caravaggio's bad luck with religious patrons in Rome. His first version of the altarpiece for the Contarelli Chapel, *The Inspiration of St Matthew* (the date is disputed, 1599–1602; formerly Berlin, destroyed) was rejected – although, it is telling that the picture was immediately purchased by Giustiniani. Moreover, in this case, Caravaggio was given another chance to complete his assignment; his second version, painted in 1602–1603, was accepted and remains *in situ*. Yet, several other pictures were rejected (one or both of the first versions of the Cerasi laterals)[24] or removed from their original location (the *Madonna dei Palafrenieri*, Galleria Borghese, Rome).[25] The *Death of the Virgin* (c. 1603, Louvre, Paris), an altarpiece for the Discalced Carmelites of Santa Maria della Scala in Trastevere, represents the most clear-cut case of Caravaggio's decorum-breaching, earthbound interpretations of divine mysteries meeting with the disapproval of ecclesiastical authorities.[26] It has been suggested that Caravaggio's violent behavior – his numerous run-ins with the law – had so badly damaged his reputation that patrons no longer wanted his works in their churches. But this is a myth built on negative remarks from biased critics.

Naples, Malta, Sicily, and Naples (The Final Years) 1606–1610

Caravaggio's Roman period came to an abrupt end when he murdered his former friend Ranuccio Tomassoni in a gang fight on 28 May 1606, the anniversary of the coronation of Pope Paul V Borghese.[27] He fled the Eternal City, never to return. The artist probably received shelter from the Colonna family in Paliano or nearby towns during the summer months before making his way to Naples – safely outside the jurisdiction of the papal authorities – by September 1606. In the nine months or so that he lived in the Spanish-controlled city, Caravaggio produced some of his most remarkable and influential altarpieces.[28] Chief among these is the *Seven Works of Mercy* (fig. 6), completed by January 1607 for the charitable confraternity of the Pio Monte della Misericordia, still *in situ*. Caravaggio's palette, which had become significantly darker in the last works in Rome (e.g., the *Madonna of Loreto* altarpiece in Sant'Agostino of c. 1605–1606), now restricts itself almost exclusively to a simple, nearly monochromatic array of dark earth tones and silvery whites. The occasional flash of red or yellow nearly jumps off the canvas. Caravaggio's brushwork is now noticeably looser and his models – poor, rough types culled from the Neapolitan streets – more realistically described than ever before.

Fig. 6. *Seven Works of Mercy,* Naples, Church of the Pio Monte della Misericordia

By 12 July 1607 Caravaggio had made his way to the island of Malta, where he sought a knighthood from the Grand Master of the Knights of St John, Alof de Wignacourt, whose rule lasted from 1601 to 1622. The artist painted a flattering full-length portrait of the Frenchman with one of his pages (Paris, Louvre; pls. I–III). For the Oratory of San Giovanni Decollato annexed to the Church of St John in Valletta (the Knights' conventual church), Caravaggio painted what many regard as his supreme masterpiece, *The Beheading of St John the Baptist* (*in situ*), in which the artist signed his name in the 'blood' oozing from the saint's severed neck (pls. VIII–XVI). This is the only work, so far as we know, that he signed in his career. Though the artist fulfilled his one-year novitiate and received his title, he committed a crime and was imprisoned. He fled Malta in late September or early October 1608 and made his way to Syracuse. He was defrocked *in absentia* by the Knights on 1 December 1608. The circumstances of his trip to Malta; the character of his patrons; and the style, meaning, and reception of the works he produced on the island are the subject of the following two chapters.

Caravaggio's brief Sicilian period, during which he moved from Syracuse to Messina and then to Palermo before returning to Naples in September or October 1609, yielded some of his most moving and inventive altarpieces. His revolutionary compositional method developed in Malta, in which a concentrated group of figures is set into a cavernous space of which the top half is left almost completely unarticulated, is made even more expressive by the austerity and compactness of his Sicilian designs. In the *Burial of St Lucy* (fig. 17) for S. Lucia al Sepolcro, Syracuse (before Dec. 1608), or the *Adoration of the Shepherds* (fig. 7) of 1609 (Museo Regionale, Messina), Caravaggio compresses his figures into a mass of humanity absorbed in a single action. Individuality has been reduced. Gestures are nearly eliminated. So thinly painted that large areas of the dark red ground are left exposed, these canvases begin a new trend that Caravaggio would not live to develop. The absorptive quality of his dark chiaroscuro in concert with the introspective glances of his actors generates a pathos unequalled in Italian painting.

Caravaggio's second Naples sojourn is not well documented other than a report of a near fatal slashing of his face by a group of armed men. Under the impression that one of his patrons had set the stage for him to receive a papal pardon, he set sail for Rome in the summer of

Fig. 7. *Adoration of the Shepherds*, Messina,
Museo Regionale

1610. However, upon arriving at Palo, he was the victim of mistaken
identity – his goods were seized and he was put in prison. Released
two days later, he contracted a fever and died soon afterwards, on
18 July, as he made his way to Port'Ercole in the hope of finding his
belongings.[29]

By the middle of the eighteenth-century, Caravaggio's art was
nearly forgotten. Though there were moments of interest in his style
by such painters as Joseph Wright of Derby (1734–97) and Jacques-
Louis David (1748–1825), Caravaggio – like most artists of the Italian
Baroque – became little more than a name in art dictionaries. It was
largely due to the writings of the great Italian scholar Roberto Longhi
(1890–1970), culminating in the pivotal exhibition he organized
in Milan in 1951 (*Mostra di Caravaggio e dei caravaggeschi*), and the

seminal monograph he published a year later,[30] that Caravaggio re-emerged as a major personality in the history of art. But one suspects even Longhi could not have anticipated the avalanche of scholarship produced on the painter in the last thirty-five years, much of it based on new documentary discoveries and technical analysis. He would not have been surprised, though, to find a book on Caravaggio in Malta. For it was Longhi himself who had baptised the *Beheading of St John* in the Oratory at Valletta 'the painting of the century'.

NOTES

1. Trans. Kitson 1967, p. 10.
2. For the police reports and related documents, see Friedlaender 1955. In addition to this important study, fundamental readings on Caravaggio's art and life also include: Gash 1980; Cinotti 1983; Hibbard 1983; *Age of Caravaggio* 1985; Moir 1989; Longhi 1992; Puglisi 1998; Langdon 1999; Marini 2001; and Spike 2001.
3. On the refused works, see Spezzaferro 2001.
4. There is a current debate amongst scholars about the question of 'autograph replicas' in Caravaggio's oeuvre. Did Caravaggio make repetitions of his own works? See Christiansen 1990.
5. The painting is lost. Marini 2002, pp. 233-42, has proposed a picture in London (private collection) as the missing portrait of the poet.
6. On Marino and Caravaggio, see Cropper 1991.
7. Moir 1967; Spear 1971; Nicolson 1989.
8. For Caravaggio's vast network of protectors, see especially Calvesi 1990; and Langdon 1999. See also chapter 2 *infra*.
9. The Council was a series of 'summit meetings' in which theologians and prelates worked out vast changes in the Roman Catholic Church as a response to the Protestant Reformation. In their last session, in 1563, they made important statements on the proper use of imagery in religious art. See *Saints and Sinners* 1999, for several essays dealing with the impact of the Catholic Reform on baroque art and iconography. See also *Genius of Rome* 2001.
10. For an exhaustive study of Caravaggio's family and connections to the town of Caravaggio and its rulers, the Sforza Colonna, see Berra 2005.
11. On Caravaggio's critics, see Mahon 1947.
12. For Caravaggio's classical sources, see Orr 1982; and Posèq 1998. Caravaggio seems to have had a love-hate relationship with his more famous namesake Michelangelo Buonarroti, whose works are frequently cited in Caravaggio's paintings (e.g., the Berlin *Amore Vincitore*). See Hibbard 1983, chapter 6; Stone 2002; and the discussion of the Pitti *Sleeping Cupid* in chapter 3 below.
13. See Freedberg 1983, for a useful comparison of the Carracci's early paintings to those of Caravaggio.
14. Giustiniani 1981, p. 42: 'il Caravaggio disse, che tanta manifattura gli era a fare un quadro buono di fiori, come di figure'.
15. Bellori 1672, transl. in Hibbard 1983, p. 372.
16. For more on Bellori's ideas, see *L'Idea del Bello* 2000; and Bell–Willette 2002.
17. The following sections of the present text are revised from Stone 2004[1].
18. See chapter 2 below.

19.   For this period, see Berra 2005, chapter 10.
20.   Puglisi 1998, chapter 1, on Caravaggio's 'Lombard Roots'.
21.   On Caravaggio's habit of painting directly from the model, see the groundbreaking article by Christiansen 1986; cf. also Gregori 1991. No drawings have been securely attributed to Caravaggio. It stands to reason that he must have made drawings occasionally, perhaps more than we suspect. Certainly he must have drawn in his youth in Lombardy. It might be that early Caravaggio drawings are close in style to those by his teacher Peterzano.
22.   Posner 1971. See also Bersani–Dutoit 1998.
23.   For recent research on the commission, see Spezzaferro 2001.
24.   Spezzaferro 2001.
25.   Rice 1997, 43–45, who argues that the picture was rejected because the Palafrenieri lost their rights to an altar in the new basilica of St Peter's, not because the nudity of the Christ Child offended the patrons. As Rice (p. 45) comments in a passage that has eluded several recent studies on the Borghese painting: 'The fate that befell Caravaggio's altarpiece seems to have resulted from a misunderstanding between the members of the Confraternity [of the Palafrenieri] and the authorities with whom they were dealing. Evidence is lacking as to how the Confraternity came to be assigned the altar in the northwest corner chapel in the first place. But apparently this occurred at the very outset of Paul's pontificate, before a policy for the distribution of the altars had been worked out. By the time the painting was installed five months later, the situation had changed. In order to guarantee the universality of the new basilica, it had been decided that private patronage, which had played so vital a part in the history of the altars in old St. Peter's, would no longer be permitted except in extraordinary cases. Once the Palafrenieri realized that they were to be deprived of their altar in St. Peter's, the altarpiece lost its usefulness to them. For that matter, it may have been they themselves who decided to take it down, preferring to sell it than to forfeit their investment by leaving it in place. In the end they even turned a profit, for Cardinal Scipione Borghese purchased the painting for 100 *scudi*, which was 25 *scudi* more than they had paid for it'.
26.   Askew 1990.
27.   See Langdon 1999, pp. 309–13.
28.   For Caravaggio's late period, see now especially London 2005, with previous bibliography.
29.   Caravaggio's death was treated as a morality play by several authors, generating further myths about the artist. See Sohm 2002.
30.   Longhi 1992 (1952 and 1968 eds.).

Fig. 8. Ottavio Leoni, *Portrait of Caravaggio*, c. 1621–5, red and black chalk with white heightening on blue paper, Florence, Biblioteca Marucelliana

CHAPTER TWO

Virtuosity honoured, Chivalry disgraced

Keith Sciberras

The fascinating and dramatic story of Caravaggio and the Knights of Malta is a brief one. It lasted for under two years, but it significantly shaped the artist's career and fortune. In Caravaggio's short life as *pictor celeberrimus*, this period between 1607 and 1608 was, indeed, a long one. In the small island of Malta, and within the powerful embrace of the Knights of the Order of St John of Jerusalem, Rhodes and Malta, Caravaggio (fig. 8) found refuge, honour, and glory, but also imprisonment and disgrace.

The Knights of Malta were the sons of the great Catholic nobility; princes from different languages living together in a chivalric embrace of brotherhood and subject directly to the Pope. This embrace was, nonetheless, marked by nationalism, family pride, and political rivalry. Religion combined with chivalry and military valour in the history of these Hospitaller Knights. Their history was five centuries old and was one of considerable turmoil. Established in the late eleventh century as Hospitallers for pilgrims in Jerusalem within the context of the Crusades, the Order of St John gradually grew into a Christian military power as they struggled against the Muslim 'infidels'.[1] Following the loss of Jerusalem, the Knights were gradually driven further away from the Holy Land, establishing themselves in Rhodes before capitulating there in 1522. After wandering through various cities for some eight years, the Knights established themselves in Malta in 1530 following the donation of the islands by the Spanish Emperor Charles V. Malta became their *Convento* and the island took up a new role as a military outpost of the Roman Catholic faith.

The Convent was first established in the Grand Harbour on the promontory spearheaded by Fort St Angelo beyond which there was

Fig. 9. Francesco Villamena, after Fra Francesco dell'Antella, *Map of Valletta*, engraving from G. Bosio, *Istoria della Sacra Religione*, vol. 3, Rome, 1602

the small town of Birgu, known as 'Vittoriosa' following the triumph in the Great Siege laid by the Turks in 1565. Fort St Angelo was on the other side of where Valletta was later to be built. In Birgu, the Knights had their own Conventual Church, located by the water's edge, and their Auberges (or inns) were dispersed within the town. But the siege of 1565 had taught the Knights a lesson; if they wanted to survive another major attack from the Turks they had to transfer their Convent onto a centrally projecting peninsula between the Harbours of Malta. This was the Xeberras promontory, which emerged between two harbours; the famous Grand Harbour was on one side and the Marsamxetto Harbour on the other side. The new city was planned according to Renaissance principles and was named after Grand Master Jean Parisot de La Valette (1557–1568), the great hero of the siege. La Valette did not however live long enough to see his new city completed.

The building and fortifications of Valletta were constructed at a fast and ambitious pace. The fortification lines, especially, were a mammoth undertaking and a physical strain for all those involved, patrons and workmen alike. This building activity coincided with a period when the Knights were probably at the peak of their fame, considering the triumphant acclaim that they had emerged with following the valorous containment of the Turks less than a decade earlier. There had been a surge in new recruits from the major Catholic houses and a feeling of well being, particularly following the role that the Knights played in Lepanto in 1571, was in the air.

In 1601, a powerful Frenchman from Picardy, Alof de Wignacourt, was elected to the Grand Magistry. Still in his early fifties, he had orchestrated his election well; his Magistry was to exceed over twenty years. Bold and tough, he would rule over Malta with both vigour and discipline. By the date of his election, Valletta had taken shape (fig. 9) and its cosmopolitan climate was ready to embrace great artists and works of art. The city was a small place, but extraordinarily cosmopolitan and fascinating. It reflected the Knights' vast international network of friends and alliances, a network that could penetrate within every corner of the Roman Catholic world. Caravaggio's Rome was obviously one of them, as was Naples.

Late in June 1607, just after the feast day of St John the Baptist, Caravaggio left Naples heading south for Malta.[2] There, Caravaggio probably believed that powerful patrons and good fortune would bring him politically closer to Rome and to papal pardon. It is still not clear what was really in the artist's mind, whether it was the search for greater protection and security, or the dream of knighthood. Yet, it may also be possible that he was attracted to the island because Wignacourt was desirous for a painter to serve his court. In Malta, Caravaggio's fortune was initially great and his first year was probably even better that he had expected. His outstanding pictures from this period are testimony of his well-being, and also of his emotional stability. Life seemed too good to be true, until all went so suddenly wrong.

Caravaggio's Maltese period is largely concerned with his knighthood, that is, his ambition for it, his arming, and disrobing (frontispiece; figs. 8, 10).[3] Before arriving in Malta he certainly knew about honorific knighthoods and knighthood may well have been one of his ambitions. He should also have known, however, that the Statutes of the Order of St John prohibited the reception of anyone guilty of murder, and certainly he would have realised that this was a great obstacle. The fact that Caravaggio had committed murder was not, however, the only hurdle that the artist needed to overcome had he really wanted to be armed with the habit of Knight of Magistral Obedience. Reserved for valorous men who did not possess noble lineage, this was the only honorific knighthood for which he would have been eligible. There had, however, been some very recent changes in their conferment and when Caravaggio set sail for Malta, the ruling Grand Master had not, ever since his election in 1601, been favourably inclined to bestow such knighthoods.[4] It is possible that Caravaggio was not aware of Wignacourt's policy on the matter; it is even probable that he did not care and that it became the Grand Master's concern when, in turn, he wanted to invest Caravaggio with the habit of Magistral Obedience. This was no easy task, and certainly not something that a Grand Master could officially promise to a fugitive from papal Rome. Thus, when Caravaggio left Naples for Malta there was probably no prior, formal, agreement with the Magistry for his election to the knighthood. Wignacourt's admiration for Caravaggio matured in Malta, after the artist had proved his worth.[5]

Caravaggio travelled to Malta on the galleys of the Order that were making their way to Malta from Naples. The fact that he travelled in style and not on one of the many private or mercantile vessels, indicates that he was no common passenger. His ability to go on board the galleys with no difficulty whatsoever – identification, passport, luggage, everything in order – provides further proof that he was the recipient of considerable protection.[6]

It should be remembered that these galleys, five of them, were under the command of General Fabrizio Sforza Colonna, who certainly knew the artist well.[7] The son of Caravaggio's staunch protector Costanza Colonna (Marchesa di Caravaggio), Fra Fabrizio, Prior of Venice and General of the Order's Galleys, had great political power and enjoyed considerable protection. Fabrizio had lived a controversial life; sent in 'privileged exile' to Malta by papal order in 1602 he returned to glory through his membership in the governing Council and his appointment as General of the Galleys in 1606. Reserved for the *Langue* of Italy, this post was indeed a fitting appointment for the grandson of the great hero of Lepanto, Marcantonio Colonna. On board the galleys in mid-June 1607, making their way into the harbours of Naples, Fabrizio had his mother Costanza, whom he had picked up from Torre del Greco.[8]

On this occasion, the galleys' stop in Naples was short, some ten days or so; they came from the North and were only passing through

Fig. 10. Anonymous, *Portrait of Caravaggio*, Mdina, Malta, Archbishop's Palace, detail

the city to gather provisions. In such circumstances, it is difficult to maintain that it was Fabrizio Sforza Colonna himself who had managed to convince Caravaggio to abruptly abandon Naples and travel with him to Malta. Everything was probably well orchestrated beforehand, with Caravaggio, having fixed his papers, probably keenly awaiting the galleys' arrival.[9] In the Order's strict military code, all the persons taken aboard had to be notified to the General; Fabrizio Sforza Colonna thereafter instructed on which of the galleys such persons were to sail.[10]

In Naples, Caravaggio's papers would have been prepared by Fra Giovanni Andrea Capeci who, as Receiver, was responsible for the provisions for the galleys. That Capeci was somehow involved in Caravaggio's passage to Malta can also be proposed on account of his earlier involvement in the failed transfer of a painter to Malta. In the early months of 1606, Wignacourt was seeking to obtain the services, from Florence, of a painter (unfortunately unnamed). Wignacourt's correspondence of March 1606 shows that negotiations were reaching a conclusion, so much so that he made provisions for the painter's voyage to Malta. The unnamed painter had to pass through Naples, and there Capeci had to assist him in buying the necessary pigments and provisions and secure his safe passage to Malta through Messina.[11] For some unknown reason, the painter did not make it to Malta. It is not known that he left Florence to take up the position. But Capeci, and the Knights of Malta in Naples, now knew how eager Wignacourt was to have a painter in his service. Caravaggio's presence in Naples was no secret. He must have seemed to these Neapolitan knights to be a perfect choice.

Caravaggio's voyage to Malta on these galleys was, as was his whole life, an adventure. This voyage was a dangerous one, because seven large enemy vessels from Barbary had just been sighted off the coast of Gozo, Malta's sister island. Wignacourt had every reason to believe that they were waiting to engage the galleys of Sforza Colonna. Five of these enemy vessels had, on 25 June, disembarked soldiers and attacked, unsuccessfully, the Order's guards on Gozo. Observing this, Wignacourt immediately warned Sforza Colonna of 'the advantage that the enemy has because of the larger number of vessels and because our galleys are burdened and with provisions in tow'.[12] Wignacourt's concern grew when, by early July, the enemy vessels were still in Maltese waters. For this reason he sent a frigate to accompany his galleys' return; he could do little more. It can be safely presumed that, in their voyage from Sicily to Malta, all men on board, including Caravaggio, were in a state of alert and armed for combat. It is a scenario in which it is not difficult to imagine Caravaggio feeling at ease, his sword firmly grasped in anticipation of combat.

The naval encounter did not, however, materialise and the galleys of the Order arrived in Malta around 12 July.[13] This was Caravaggio's first view of Valletta (fig. 11). Against a backdrop of glowing limestone, Caravaggio would have also noted the macabre sight of the gallows, so prominently exposed to greet the visitors on the first promontory on the left of the harbour; this was a daunting reminder of the Order's

Fig. 11. *Fort St Angelo from Ricasoli Point*

rule of law. Within the harbour, on the third promontory on the left was Fort St Angelo, where many glorious episodes of the Great Siege of 1565 had unfolded; it was now, among other things, a prison for unruly knights.

In the corridors of power within the palace of the Grand Master in Valletta, Caravaggio's former patrons in Rome were frequently mentioned; the Mattei, Costa, Giustiniani and Sforza Colonna had established intimate ties with Wignacourt and were in correspondence with him. The Borghese papal family was obviously much revered. News that Caravaggio was in Malta would have spread fast. Many probably did not even know who the artist was, but a select few were distinguished 'cognoscenti' and were powerful enough to canvass in his favour with the Grand Master. The Grand Master was probably expecting him, perhaps as a replacement for the artist who should have arrived through Naples in 1606.

Caravaggio attracted around him prominent personalities, and his circle of protectors grew to include new patrons, among whom were Francesco dell'Antella and Ippolito Malaspina, for whom he painted the easel pictures of *Sleeping Cupid* (pl. XVII; Florence, Palazzo Pitti) [14]

23

Fig. 12. *St Jerome Writing*, Valletta, Museum of St John's, detail: Malaspina arms and profile of 1661 frame

and *St Jerome Writing* (pl. IV, Valletta, St John's Museum).[15] A further patron – probably rather than securely – was Antonio Martelli, who is likely to be the person painted in the *Portrait of a Knight* (pl. XX, Florence, Palazzo Pitti).[16]

A Florentine, Fra Francesco dell'Antella was personal assistant and secretary to Wignacourt. Erudite and a man of culture, he moved within the innermost circles of the Grand Master, also apparently occupying the role of what can be called the 'consultant for culture and the arts'. Knight of Malta since 1587, he was young, influential, talented, and sophisticated; he was a person who was immediately to take advantage of Caravaggio's presence on the island. The *Sleeping Cupid*, painted as a private piece, is indeed a brilliant reflection of the sophistication of dell'Antella's taste.

A cousin of the great Admiral Gian Andrea Doria, Fra Ippolito Malaspina, Marchese di Fosdinovo, was a political heavyweight of the older generation and the former General of the Papal Galleys under Clement VIII (fig. 12). Related to Ottavio Costa (patron of great works such as the *Conversion of the Magdalene*, *Judith and Holofernes*, and the *Ecstasy of St Francis*) through the latter's marriage, he had lived in Rome as General of the Papal Galleys precisely at the time Caravaggio achieved public recognition there and when he was painting pictures for Costa; Malaspina may have been acquainted with the artist. The Marchese was great uncle to Costa's sons Alessandro and Antonio Costa, both Knights of St John, who later were responsible for the beautiful tomb slab dedicated to Malaspina in the centre of the floor of the Chapel of the Italian Langue in St John's Conventual Church, Valletta.

A Conventual Bailiff, occupying the dignity of the Bailiwick of St. John of Naples (San Giovanni a Mare), and intimate adviser to Grand Master Wignacourt, as well as a knight with a glorious military career, Malaspina had been away from Malta for some four years before returning in July 1607 on the very same galleys that had brought the artist.[17] It seems that, on the same galleys, there was also Alessandro Costa who was heading to Malta to be enlisted as a Page to the Grand Master.[18] Caravaggio's painting of *St Jerome* was a private commission, probably intended to hang in Malaspina's own house in Valletta (it was donated to the chapel of Italy in St John's Conventual Church after his death in 1624; figs. 13, 14). It probably dates to early 1608, painted in a moment of considerable reflection, precisely when the artist had again a climate of security and was looking forward to a new reality.

A member of the illustrious Florentine family of the Martelli, Fra Antonio Martelli had a particularly brilliant military career, initiated with his participation in the Great Siege of 1565. In the following three decades he participated in numerous campaigns with the Order, the Venetian fleet and at the service of the Grand Duke of Tuscany. Present in Malta during the early years of the seventeenth century, Martelli was one of the most senior Italian knights, occupying the post of Lieutenant to the Admiral on more than one occasion. The Admiral was the head (or *pilier*) of the Italian knights. Elected Prior of Hungary in 1603, he subsequently renounced this position in 1605 to become Admiral. In October 1606, past seventy years of age, he took up the dignity of Prior of Messina.

Fig. 13. *Chapel of Italy with 'St Jerome Writing'* (*in situ* with Malaspina's tomb in the centre of the floor), Valletta, St John's Co-Cathedral

It is clearly documented that Martelli was in Malta throughout Caravaggio's stay on the island and that, for the first two years of his tenure as Prior of Messina, he kept residence in Malta and administered his priory through procurators. The use of lieutenants was standard practice in the Order. During this period he also maintained vital business relations with Florence. He had been granted licence to move to his Priory in Messina already in March 1608 but did not exercise it until several months later; he was actually in Malta until late October 1608 and was in Messina by 4 November.[19] In Caravaggio's painting, the knight is represented wearing an informal monastic black habit with a large eight pointed cross on his chest. This was, primarily, the habit of the Grand Crosses of the Order. It was not the first picture that Caravaggio had painted on the island. The first three months were the hot months of summer; the knight is here wearing a thick habit with a long shirt beneath.

To these Italian patrons should be added the members of the Lorraine family. Charles of Lorraine, Conte de Brie, was in Malta, amid initial controversy, throughout 1608,[20] precisely when his father Henry II assumed the title of Duke of Lorraine following the death of Charles II. Natural born, but out of wedlock, Charles de Brie had been official recognised in 1605, just before Henry's second marriage to Margerita Gonzaga. Carrying the political power of the Lorraines, he was immediately induced into becoming a Knight of Malta.[21] Present also was Prince Francis of Lorraine, brother of Henry II, who came to the island with great pomp for a short spell late in July 1608.[22] This was likely the most appropriate opportunity for the Lorraine family to commission the *Annunciation of the Virgin* (pl. XXII) shortly afterwards donated by Henry II to the primatial church of Nancy.[23] The painting remains unfortunately undocumented but, stylistically, it fits remarkably well within the corpus of the period in question.

It is clear that, upon landing, Caravaggio had enough acquaintances who could offer to host him, at least temporarily, at their residence. Malaspina's house was on the Salvatore bastion overlooking Marsamxetto, Sforza Colonna had his own residence, and Marc'Aurelio Giustiniani, cousin of Marchese Vincenzo Giustiniani and of Cardinal Benedetto, was also on the island. Yet, it is not known where Caravaggio resided in Malta; he may have stayed with one of his protectors or in one of the inns at Valletta.[24]

The first reference to Caravaggio in Malta is a chance reference from the Inquisitors' Archives.[25] On 14 July, that is, immediately following his arrival, Caravaggio attended a welcome party given by Giacomo Marchese, a Sicilian knight who had embarked on the same galleys during their stop at Messina. At the party Marchese was overheard talking about a Greek painter who kept two wives. This attracted the attention of Judge Paolo Cassar, who was also present and who conscientiously reported the matter to the Inquisitor Leonetto Corbiaro. The latter opened an enquiry and Caravaggio was summoned before his court on July 26. At the Inquisitor's questioning the artist responded evasively, saying that he did not know anything about what had been said: '*Io di questo che me dimanda . . . non so cosa alcuna*'. Giacomo Marchese was called to testify weeks later, on 18 September. He also said that he did not know anything about the matter and declared that the entire situation had arisen out of an innocent joke. The enquiry failed to reach any conclusion. It looked as if the story had been an innocent, if not so harmless joke, but it does provide evidence that Caravaggio was well and truly physically in Malta.

The weeks that followed Caravaggio's arrival in Malta are still biographically hazy, but the artist was beginning to gain considerable prestige. This was the start of a context that would see the artist's virtuosity honoured. Grand Master Wignacourt gradually came to realise his good fortune; perhaps he heard stories of how Italian princes, cardinals and bankers sought to have him in their service. Around this time Wignacourt had himself portrayed in full armour, accompanied by a page. The painting now hangs in the Louvre, Paris (pl. I).[26] It is probably one of the first paintings by Caravaggio in Malta, a test piece that set the scene for the greater glory the artist was to achieve on the island.

The Grand Master and his close collaborators recognised the benefits that the Order could reap from Caravaggio's presence. They were aware that an artist of such talent, courted by many, would not stay long on the island unless he was offered a prize beyond monetary payment, a prize that was hard to refuse. In the Palace corridors, they now began planning on how to keep him in Malta or permanently associated with the Order. The Grand Master had a number of alternatives. The simplest was to elect Caravaggio as a member of the palace household, giving him all the privileges that it carried. There had been a recent case in point; some twelve years earlier Grand

Fig. 14. *St John's Co-Cathedral* (Oratory roof visible at right), Valletta

Master Martino Garzes had done the same with the Florentine painter Filippo Paladini, who was a convicted criminal and who had arrived in Malta as a galley slave.[27] Wignacourt, however, wanted an even more intimate connection and opted for a bold move. He would make Caravaggio a knight. This was an honour that was to the advantage of both artist and patron.

However, as noted earlier, Wignacourt himself had abolished the Knighthood of Magistral Obedience, the knighthood to which Caravaggio would have been eligible. In the Order's ranking, the Knighthood of Magistral Obedience was primarily an honorific conferment and had little political stature. Such knights, however, still had to wear the black and white habit, enjoyed a small pension, and food and accommodation when in residence in the convent. Even though socially prestigious, the knighthood was of less importance than the Knighthood of Grace, where a degree of nobility was required, and obviously much less important than that of Justice. The latter was reserved for true noble knights. Knights of Magistral Obedience, however, still required to be regularly professed 'in Convent' and normally had to spend a full year in residence as novices.

Wignacourt's desire to keep the artist was considerable; determined to make him a knight he needed, however, Papal support in order to go beyond the dictates of the Order's own statutes. The Grand Master needed two papal dispensations in favour of a man who was, ironically, fleeing from papal authority. One was for investing a man who had committed murder, and the other for making him a Knight of Magistral Obedience. In a letter of 29 December 1607, Wignacourt wrote to his Ambassador in Rome, Fra Francesco Lomellini, and briefed him on this request, which was in turn to be addressed to the papal court. He did not mention Caravaggio by name, but referred to him as a 'person of great virtues, honourable, and respectful, and whom we particularly respect as our servitor'.[28] Moreover, he explains his desire by his wish 'not to lose' him (*per non perderlo*). And it is precisely this fear of losing him that would have been the principal motive for Caravaggio's arming as a knight. Once a knight, Caravaggio could not leave Malta without the Grand Master's consent. To assist Lomellini in his request to the papacy, Wignacourt enrolled the help of the powerful *letterato* Giacomo Bosio, who was similarly informed by a letter of 29 December.[29] Lomellini and, more importantly, Bosio acted immediately and papal authority was granted on 7 February 1608.[30] This was, remarkably, a mere three weeks or so after receipt of the Grand Master's letter in Rome. The full document of the authorisation, as released by the papacy, is dated 15 February 1608.[31]

In other words, by the end of February, the Grand Master would have received the news from his Ambassador. The news spread fast within the Palace corridors. Caravaggio himself would have been summoned by the Grand Master and informed that there were no longer any difficulties with his admission into the Order. Less than two years after murdering Ranuccio Tomassoni, some eight months after he left Naples, a new chapter in his life was to begin. His only remaining obligation was that of fulfilling the requirements of a year's residence 'in Convent' as a novice prior to his arming. Wignacourt was obviously desirous for a speedy outcome. It can be inferred, from the date of Caravaggio's admission, that the Grand Master gave instructions to have his year counted immediately after his arrival in Malta. He could thus be armed in mid-July 1608.

Caravaggio's thoughts would, at this stage, certainly have turned to Rome. After all, the concessions made by Paul V represented a major step towards pardon. In Malta, Caravaggio thus found himself building a strong foundation for his eventual return to Rome; a return that certainly could not have been foreseen had he, a fugitive for the crime of murder, reappeared 'triumphantly' as a knight of the Order of Malta, armed and wearing the black habit with the white eight-pointed cross proudly exhibited over his shoulder (fig. 10).

The reception ceremony at which Caravaggio was invested with the habit of a Knight of Magistral Obedience was held on 14 July 1608. The Grand Master thus fulfilled his wish 'to gratify the desire of this excellent painter, so that our island of Malta, and our Order may at last glory in this adopted disciple and citizen with no less pride than the island of Kos (also within our jurisdiction) extols her Apelles; and that, should we compare him to more recent artists of our age, we may not afterwards be envious of the artistic excellence of some other man, outstanding in his art, whose name and brush are equally important'.[32] Admiration for Caravaggio's work is deliberately spelled out, as are the expectations that his art was to be a vehicle for the glorification of the Knights of Malta. Virtuosity was being honoured.

At his first opportunity, Caravaggio proudly signed his name as Fra Michael Angelo, painted in the blood oozing from Saint John's head in the *Beheading of Saint John the Baptist*, painted as an altarpiece for the Oratory of San Giovanni Decollato attached to the Conventual Church in Valletta (pl. VIII). This great picture is a monument to artistic discipline, to how the artist arranges space and controls the gestures and actions of such a brutal scene. It is a picture studied with mathematical precision, an intellectual *componimento* rendered with outstanding realism. This is the most impressive moment of Caravaggio in Malta, a picture made as an expression of virtue. His signature is precisely at its centre and he does not fail to declare his new social status: Michelangelo, Knight of Malta.

As a Knight of Malta, Caravaggio's social life took on an entirely new dimension; he was now bound by obedience, respect for his superiors, and by the strict observance of the Statutes of the Order. Long hours in taverns, brawls, blasphemy, gaming, the colourful aspects of street life and consorting with prostitutes were to become a thing of the past. He was now obliged to be decorous in his demeanour and to wear his habit with dignity and composure. But Valletta was a cosmopolitan city and temptations were around every corner;[33] Caravaggio's turbulent nature could not be contained for too long.

Chivalry was to be disgraced barely four weeks later. A brawl was to lead to his disgrace.

It happened in Valletta on the night of 18 August 1608.[34] The circumstances emerge with some clarity, even if it is still difficult to explain what led up to it. A fight broke out in the house of the organist of the Conventual Church of St John, Fra Prospero Coppini, who, however, does not seem to have taken an active part. The fight was no small affair and seven knights, all Italians, were involved. Arms were used, and a shot was fired. The front door of Coppini's residence was smashed and broken open and one of the knights, Fra Giovanni Rodomonte Roero, Conte della Vezza di Asti, was seriously wounded. The Venerable Council was immediately notified and an investigation was set up the following day. Caravaggio and Fra Giovanni Pietro de Ponte, a deacon of the Conventual Church, were the first among the perpetrators to be identified, on 27 August 1608,[35] by the Criminal Commission. Both men would have been put in detention in Fort St Angelo immediately afterwards.[36] This was only two days before the feast of San Giovanni Decollato, when Caravaggio's monumental picture was probably to be unveiled in the Oratory of the Decollato.[37]

Caravaggio seems to have spent September 1608, or the greater part of it, detained in Fort St Angelo (fig. 15).[38] This was a large and now somewhat derelict fort, but it had had a glorious past, holding the Order's standard during the memorable months of the Great Siege. Its military significance had diminished with the building of Valletta, but nonetheless it still offered an imposing sight in the harbour. In St Angelo, unable to paint, it was inevitable, given the artist's temperament, that his inventiveness was kept alive by planning his incredible escape. Caravaggio's break-out, incredible as it still seems, took place in early October and must have been the successful outcome of an elaborate plot. He was, once again, on the run. Obviously, his brush and pigments were probably left behind.

On 6 October 1608, the Venerable Council was informed that the Knight Fra Michelangelo Merisi da Caravaggio, while detained in Fort St Angelo, had escaped and secretly fled from the island. By this flight Caravaggio had seriously breached the Order's Statutes and one of its central points of honour and discipline.[39] It eventually led to the *privatio habitus* ceremony of 1 December 1608 (nearly two months after his escape) during which the artist was deprived of his habit

Fig. 15. *Fort St Angelo c. 1608* (reconstruction by S. Spiteri, 2004)

and expelled from the Order *in absentia*.[40] He had, through his flight, indirectly admitted his guilt for the brawl and was thus removed from the list of knights eventually tried for the affray.[41]

There has been much speculation on how Caravaggio escaped; what is known is that he used a rope (fig. 16). It is, however, difficult to establish the exact sequence of events partly because it is not clear where he was being kept within the fort. It is improbable that Caravaggio was detained, as traditionally held, in the rock-cut *guva* within the fort. He was on preventative custody and not yet condemned, thus he possibly enjoyed a certain degree of liberty within the fort's perimeter,[42] making escape easier. The main difficulty lay in getting out of Malta. At this stage, Caravaggio was certainly helped to arrive speedily in Sicily, to be greeted there by the painter friend Mario Minniti. He must somehow have secretly boarded a boat, possibly the *speronara* of a daring and corruptible boatman. Sailing through the narrow opening of the Grand Harbour would have been too much of a risk and he was probably picked up from one of the island's many bays after spending some hours, or even days, in hiding.[43] Some sixteen hours later, with favourable winds and sea, he should have been in Sicily and heading for Syracuse.

That there was an 'arrangement' to help Caravaggio escape is clear but it is difficult to ascertain who helped him. In an island of informers and of rewards for information, it is significant that nothing came of the investigations carried out by the Criminal Commission. Escaping from the Convent was, as already noted, a dishonourable deed, and a dangerous one too. Moreover, everyone in Malta knew that, in such circumstances, even the fugitive's accomplices risked a great deal, as was the case in a similar incident that happened less than a month before Caravaggio's escape. Caravaggio's accomplices, therefore, knew what they were risking.[44] If they were knights, they risked the *privatio habitus* themselves. If secular, they were also in great trouble, and liable for punishment.

But, dramatic as it was, Caravaggio's escape was not an isolated episode. During Wignacourt's magistry, other knights had fled the island or left without authorisation. In some instances, Wignacourt's furious reaction is documented. What usually happened in such cases was that the Grand Master promptly wrote to all his Receivers in the major European cities and ordered the immediate recapture and detainment of the fugitive knight.[45] It clearly emerges that the Grand Master wanted fugitives back in Malta. This would have been the situation which faced Caravaggio after his escape, and Bellori himself records that Caravaggio feared that the knights were after him.[46]

Unfortunately, specific documents confirming that Caravaggio was being pursued do not exist (though this is hinted at by biographers). But in view of the manner in which he was expelled from the Order, it does not appear that he would have been given preferential treatment and simply let go. The Order's Receivers in Sicily would have been informed about his escape, but made no move to apprehend him. Perhaps this was because Caravaggio had managed to obtain protection immediately upon his arrival on that island. It is obvious that he had important contacts and that, for the Order, his apprehension could have become an embarrassing affair. It should also be noted that, during the same period, the Order was in litigation with the Senate of Messina.[47] In such circumstances it seems that it would have been difficult for the Order to expect official help from that city; this is where Caravaggio proceeded to late in 1608 (or early 1609) after painting the dramatic *Burial of St Lucy* in Syracuse (fig. 17; Museo di Palazzo Bellomo, Syracuse).

Fig. 16. *Beheading of St John the Baptist,* Valletta, Oratory of San Giovanni Decollato, detail

That Caravaggio truly feared that he was being pursued, as suggested by his biographers, should not be excluded, because he certainly knew how Wignacourt treated those who contravened the Statutes. Moreover, throughout his first weeks in Sicily, the galleys of the Order were sailing off the harbours of that island and, whilst painting his great pictures there, he would probably have seen them from the ports where he took refuge. These galleys were a veritable reminder of the Order's vengeance and also an indirect threat. First under Sforza

Fig. 17. *Burial of St Lucy*, Syracuse, Santa Lucia al Sepolcro, on deposit at Galleria Regionale, Palazzo Bellomo

Colonna and later, after November 1608, under Francesco Moletti, the galleys were known to have been in the waters of Messina. Meanwhile, some time before 4 November, Fra Antonio Martelli arrived in Messina to take up residence as prior of the city.[48] With his presence in Messina, certainly till late summer 1609 (thus running parallel to Caravaggio's own stay), there was undoubtedly a strange and awkward situation. Martelli, as we have said, was one of the most powerful and deeply respected knights within the Order and, probably he was also one of Caravaggio's protectors in Malta. The most crucial period for the apprehension of Caravaggio by the knights in Sicily was when the Order was compiling evidence for his trial in Malta. It is during this

Fig. 18. W. Kilian, *The Criminal Tribunal in the Oratory*, engraving from C. von Osterhausen, *Eigentlicher und gründlicher Bericht . . .*, Augsburg, 1650; Washington, D.C., Catholic University of America

period that the Order would have concentrated its resources on his recapture and forced return to the Convent.[49]

In absentia, with the artist in Sicily, the trial in Malta happened on 27 November 1608. There, the Venerable Council heard details of how Caravaggio had escaped from the fort using a rope and decided that it should proceed with his disgracing and defrocking from the chivalric Order of St John.[50] It also heard and judged the criminal case for the August brawl. The Council condemned another four Italian knights to imprisonment and Caravaggio's unruly companion, the knight de Ponte, to be similarly defrocked and expelled in a ceremony that would take place four days later.[51]

On 1 December 1608, nearly two months after the artist's escape, the expulsion and defrocking of Caravaggio and de Ponte took place in the Oratory of the Decollato (fig. 18). In a twist of irony, this *privatio habitus* ceremony happened paradoxically in front of the *Beheading of Saint John the Baptist* and in the presence of the members of the Venerable Council that included most of Caravaggio's former protectors. With little respect to artistic virtue, the first to be expelled *tanquam membrum putridum et foetidum* and defrocked, *in absentia* and after a unanimous vote against him, was Fra Michelangelo Merisi da Caravaggio.[52]

NOTES

1. For the history of the Knights in English, see: Vertot 1728; Bradford 1972; Sire 1994.
2. For Caravaggio in Malta see: Farrugia Randon 1989, esp. Azzopardi 1989[1] and 1989[2]; Cutajar 1989; Calvesi 1990; Macioce 1994; Gash 1997; Stone 1997[1]; Stone 1997[2]; Florence 1999; Langdon 1999; Pacelli 1999; Macioce 2001; Marini 2001; Sciberras 2002[1]; Sciberras 2002[2]; Sciberras–Stone 2004; Farrugia Randon 2004; Sciberras 2005[2]; Sciberras–Stone 2005[1]; Sciberras–Stone 2005[2].
3. Caravaggio is represented wearing the habit of a Knight of Malta in a drawing portrait of him attributed to Ottavio Leoni (Ajaccio, private collection) and in an anonymous painting in the Bishop's Palace, Mdina, Malta (fig. 10). Another version of this painting is in a private collection. Bellori published a portrait of Caravaggio wearing an eight-pointed cross, symbol of the Order of St John, in his *Vite*. In the famous portrait by Leoni in Florence (fig. 8) there are what might be faint traces of an eight-pointed cross on Caravaggio's shoulder.
4. The Knighthood of Magistral Obedience was abolished during the 1603 a.i. [1604] Chapter General. Sciberras 2002[2], p. 16; *Le Ordinationi del Capitolo Generale celebrato nell'anno MDCIII*, Rome 1609, p. 23: De Receptione Fratrum, 10. Wignacourt himself had spoken about the numerous requests concerning this knighthood in his letter requesting a papal decree in favour of Caravaggio, and had explained how 'si fusse troppo allargata la mano massime in tempo dell'Illustrissimo Verdala, fu ne suddetto Capitolo Generale fatta l'Ordinatione e confermata dal nostro tenore dell'alligata copia, la quale per essere veramente utile, e necessaria, non habbiamo mai voluto, che si deroghi, ancor'che cene sieno state fatte molte instanze'. Letter dated 29 December 1607, in Macioce 1994, p. 207. There are similar references in the Apostolic Brief published in Azzopardi 1989[2], pp. 49–56.
5. In order to invest Caravaggio, the Grand Master required two concessions from Paul V. He needed a concession in arming a person who had committed murder and a concession in arming a Knight of Magistral Obedience. See Sciberras 2002[2], pp. 16–17. An indication of this is the date when Wignacourt sent his first request for such concessions to the pope. This was in December 1607. Had there been prior agreement, Wignacourt would no doubt have commenced the entire mechanism much earlier. Instead he waited for more than five months before putting pen to paper.
6. Sciberras 2002[2], p. 15.
7. See Calvesi 1990, pp. 131–4; Macioce 1994.
8. Denunzio 2005, p. 49.
9. The circle of Neapolitan personages who could have instilled in Caravaggio a desire for the Order of Malta should not be restricted to the Carafas and Colonnas but can be enlarged to a number of aristocratic families who had a close and intimate contact with the Order. Mention should be here made of families associated with the Pio Monte della Misericordia whom Caravaggio knew, such as the Sersale, d'Alessandro and Piscicello. Another important family was that of the Capeci, who had a long-standing tradition of

being the Order's Receivers in Naples, and they counted numerous knights. See Sciberras 2002², pp. 14–15.

10.   Sciberras 2002², p. 14. *Gli Statuti della Sac. Religione di S.Giovanni Gierosolimitano*, Rome 1609, p. 251: De Triremibus, 83.

11.   '… non mancherete d'assistere per essere egli nuovo in cotesto Paese, come per assicurarvi, che ci farete piacere acuttisimo ad aiutarlo, e consiglirlo in tutto quello, che gli potesse occorrere, particolarmente per fargli godere buon' passaggio fino a Messina …', in Stone 1997², p. 170.

12.   '… vantaggio che mostrano i nimici con più numero di vasselli che quelli della Religione come anco per presupporre che le Galere sieno assai imbarazzati, et con il remorchio', in Sciberras 2002², pp. 15–16.

13.   The date of the galleys' return to Malta is not precisely documented but it would have been in those days. Sforza Colonna's galleys would have entered the Grand Harbour amid fanfare and celebrations. They had been long awaited and were laden with provisions.

14.   See Sebregondi Fiorentini 1982; Stone 1997². See also Naples 2004, cat. no. 8 (entry by L. Sebregondi), and Chapter 3 below.

15.   See Sciberras–Stone 2005² and also Chapter 3 below.

16.   Gash 1997. See also Naples 2004, cat. no. 9 (entry by K. Sciberras–D.M. Stone) and Chapter 3 below.

17.   Macioce 1994, p. 225.

18.   Sciberras–Stone 2005².

19.   Sciberras 2002², pp. 11–12.

20.   He had been identified by Calvesi 1990, p. 375, and Macioce 1994, pp. 208–12, as the second prospective knight nominated in Paul V's Brief granted in favour of Caravaggio and another person. For the identity of the 'seconda persona', see Sciberras 2005².

21.   Henry II 'Le Bon' had two illegitimate sons, Henri (Abbot of St Michel and Pierremont) and Charles (Conte de Brie). He had married Catherine of Navarre in 1599, but had no issue. She died in 1604. In 1604, he formally recognised and legitimised both Henri and Charles. Henry II married Margerita Gonzaga in 1606. They had two issues, Nicoletta and Claudia.

22.   Calvesi 1990, p. 375; Macioce 1994, 220. AOM, Arch 102, Liber Conciliorum, f. 122*v*.

23.   Macioce 1994; Marini 2001, pp. 557–8; Sciberras 2005².

24.   Sforza Colonna is documented to have had his own residence (Notarial Archives Valletta, R.309 Not. Lorenzo Grima V.10 (1605–6), ff.175*v*–180*r*). Marc'Aurelio Giustiniani, cousin of Marchese Vincenzo Giustiniani and of Cardinal Benedetto, was also on the island, see Macioce 1994, p. 217.

25.   The documents for this case were discovered by Azzopardi. For a full transcription see Azzopardi 1978, pp. 16–20; Azzopardi 1989¹, pp. 25–31.

26.   For a detailed bibliography and a discussion of the painting see Chapter 3 below.

27.   See Sciberras–Stone 2001.

28.   '… una persona virtuosissima e di honoratissime qualità, e costumi e che tenghiamo per servitore nostro particolare', in Macioce 1994, pp. 207–8.

29.   Macioce 1994, p. 208.

30.   Azzopardi 1989², pp. 45–56

31.   Azzopardi 1989², p. 56.

32.   For the documents see Azzopardi 1989¹, pp. 32–33.

33.   Valletta was also a violent city, full of young nobles from various Langues, arrogant and difficult to contain. Duels and violence were the order of the day. 'È impossibile', wrote Wignacourt to the pope, 'che in un luogo dove si fa tanta professione d'arme, e si sta tanto in sul'punto dell'honore come qui non manchino delle volte, anzi spesso, delle risse' (see Sciberras 2002², p. 5). For a man of such a tumultuous nature as Caravaggio, Malta was thus a dangerous place.

34.   Sciberras 2002¹, p. 229.

35.   Sciberras 2002¹, p. 229.

36.   The fact that Caravaggio was detained indicates that his participation in the brawl was serious enough to be subject to a *privatio habitus* case, and that he thus risked expulsion from the Order. If it was not so, Caravaggio would have been allowed to roam free in

Malta while awaiting the criminal proceedings and trial.

37. Sciberras 2002[1], p. 231. It is probable, however, that instead of participating in the colourful pageantry associated with the celebration of the feast, Caravaggio was facing imminent arrest (if not already under arrest). Meanwhile, on 9 September, for the first time, a *privatio habitus* ceremony was held in the Oratory of the Decollato, in front of Caravaggio's painting. The knight in question was being deprived of his habit because he had escaped from Malta without the Grand Master's permission. Caravaggio probably heard of this, and thought that the same could happen to him. AOM, Arch.210, Decreta Concilio, p. 351.

38. Azzopardi 1989[1], p. 36.

39. The flight of a knight from Malta – or even unauthorised leave from the island – was a forbidden act, contravening Statute 13 of the chapter Prohibitions and Penalties. In these circumstances, the Venerable Council had to be immediately informed and a Criminal Commission was then nominated to investigate the events. This, as is well known, is what happened in Caravaggio's case on 6 October.

40. Azzopardi 1989[2], pp. 38–39.

41. Sciberras 2002[1], p. 229.

42. See Sciberras 2002[2], p. 7.

43. Sciberras 2002[2], pp. 7–8.

44. Sciberras 2002[2], pp. 8–10.

45. It is significant how, in these circumstances, Wignacourt usually asked his Receivers to capture fugitives with the greatest secrecy. This procedure was also noted in the Statute 12 of Prohibitions and Penalties which exhorted all knights to capture and detain in the prisons of their priories those knights who were wandering in that land without specific authorisation (i.e. fugitives). Even more specific are the Statutes referring to the manner of celebrating the *privatio habitus in absentia* which specifically refer to occasions when the fugitive 'could not be apprehended'. This statutory reference specifically implies that attempts should have been made to apprehend the fugitive. See Sciberras 2002[2], pp. 8–10.

46. 'Ma la disgrazia di Michele non l'abbandonava, e 'l timore lo scacciava di luogo in luogo'. See Hibbard 1983, p. 370.

47. Sciberras 2002[2], p. 10.

48. Sciberras 2002[2], pp. 10–14.

49. The fact that, after his expulsion from the Order, he seems to have lived with relative tranquillity at Messina, indicates that probably there was not a civil case pending against him in Malta. Thus, after the *privatio habitus*, his juridical case could have been considered concluded. The victim, Fra Giovanni Rodomonte Roero, had left the island. AOM, Arch. 456, Liber Bullarum, f. 156r.

50. Azzopardi 1989[1], p. 36.

51. De Ponte was later identified as the ringleader; he was armed at night and carried a pistol. De Ponte was also identified as the person who inflicted serious wounds on Fra Giovanni Rodomonte Roero. Because of the gravity of his actions, de Ponte was deprived of his habit, alongside Caravaggio, on 1 December 1608, following the trial held on 27 November. In the same trial, two novices, the Noble Giovanni Pecci and the Noble Francesco Benzo were condemned to four and two years imprisonment respectively, while the knights Fra Giulio Accarigi and Fra Giovanni Battista Scaravello were each sentenced to six months imprisonment for their involvement in the brawl. Sciberras 2002[1], pp. 230–1.

52. See Azzopardi 1989[1], pp. 38–39. See also Sammut 1978.

PLATES

I. *Portrait of Alof de Wignacourt and a Page*, Paris, Louvre

II. *Portrait of Alof de Wignacourt and a Page*, Paris, Louvre, detail

III. *Portrait of Alof de Wignacourt and a Page*, Paris, Louvre, detail

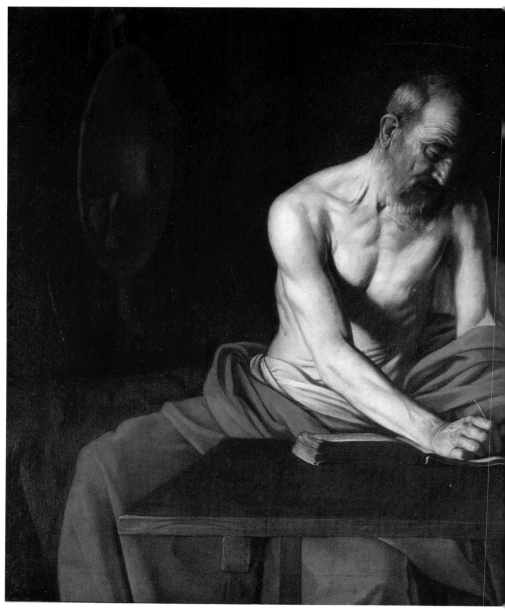

IV. *St Jerome Writing*, Valletta, Museum of St John's

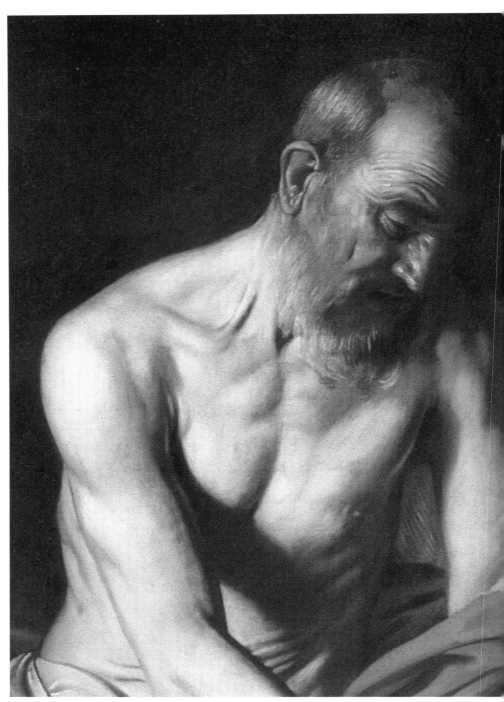

V. *St Jerome Writing*, Valletta, Museum of St John's, detail

VI. *St Jerome Writing*, Valletta, Museum of St John's, detail

VII. *St Jerome Writing*, Valletta, Museum of St John's, detail

VIII. *Oratory of San Giovanni Decollato*, Valletta, St John's Co-Cathedral

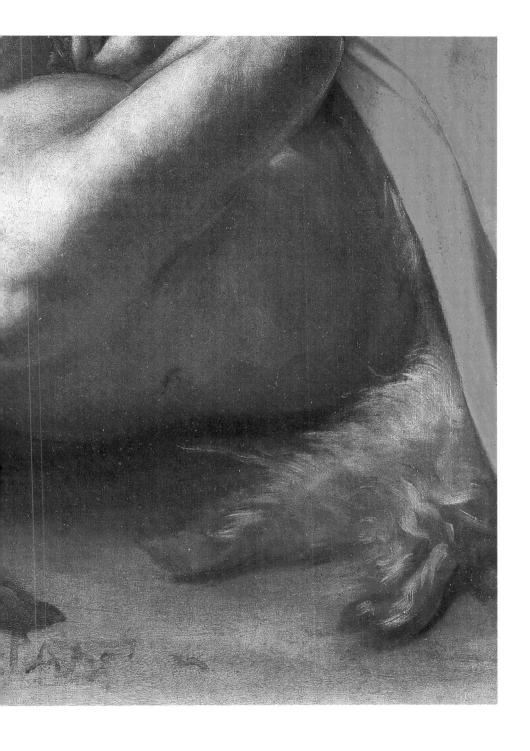

XI. *Beheading of St John the Baptist*, Valletta,
Oratory of San Giovanni Decollato, detail

XII. *Beheading of St John the Baptist*, Valletta,
Oratory of San Giovanni Decollato, detail

XIII. *Beheading of St John the Baptist,* Valletta,
Oratory of San Giovanni Decollato, detail

XIV. *Beheading of St John the Baptist*, Valletta,
Oratory of San Giovanni Decollato, detail

XV. *Beheading of St John the Baptist*, Valletta,
Oratory of San Giovanni Decollato, detail

XVI. *Beheading of St John the Baptist*, Valletta,
Oratory of San Giovanni Decollato, detail

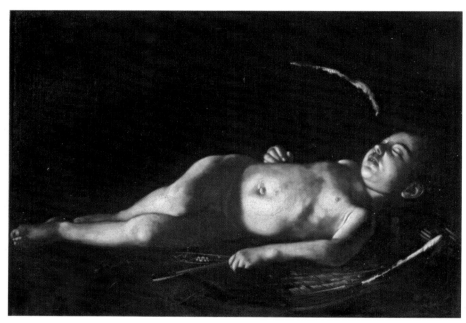

XVII. *Sleeping Cupid*, Florence, Pitti Palace

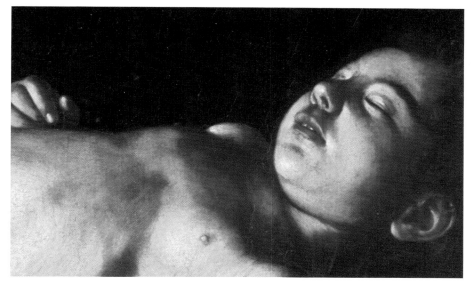

XVIII. *Sleeping Cupid*, Florence, Pitti Palace, detail

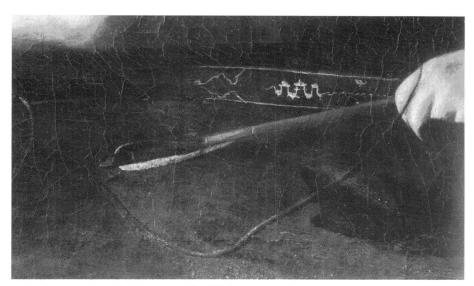

XIX. *Sleeping Cupid*, Florence, Pitti Palace, detail

XX. *Portrait of a Knight (Fra Antonio Martelli?)*, Florence, Pitti Palace

XXI. *Portrait of a Knight (Fra Antonio Martelli?)*, Florence, Pitti Palace, detail

XXII. *Annunciation*, Nancy, Musée des Beaux-Arts

CHAPTER THREE

'Fra Michelangelo' and the Art of Knighthood

David M. Stone

When Caravaggio took his first steps on Maltese soil in July 1607,[1] Valletta's new buildings – behemoths designed by the engineer who planned its fortifications – already contained several important paintings by Matteo Perez d'Aleccio and Filippo Paladini.[2] But in the summer of 1607, huge expanses in the Grand Master's palace (fig. 19) and St John's church (fig. 14) were still relatively bare.[3] Annexed to the church, the Oratory of San Giovanni Decollato (fig. 18; pl. VIII), which had only been built a couple of years earlier, in c. 1602–05, was similarly incomplete in its decoration.[4] The Order, no doubt, was counting on Merisi to lend prestige and beauty to these new sites. Indeed, it is likely that Caravaggio was invited to the island specifically to serve – for the first time in his career – as court painter.

Just as Giorgione's and Titian's paintings respond to the dappled light and watery brew of colours emanating from Venice's palace-lined canals, Caravaggio's Maltese works have an austerity and tectonic rigour that match the character of this rocky island, with its cubist panorama and stalwart military commanders (figs. 11, 20). The pictures Caravaggio painted during his fifteen-month sojourn on the island demonstrate his sensitivity to his surroundings – not only to the topography but also to the visual and spiritual culture of his knightly audience. His canvases are experimental in many ways, taking standard themes and reinventing them.

Caravaggio's Maltese works have a distinctive look. They are noticeably harder, more spartan and subdued than anything that came before them. It was here, more than in Naples, that he began to paint very economically, putting in the 'treble' highlights in a few rapid strokes, and using the reddish ground, not only as a kind of

Fig. 19. *Grand Master's Palace* (with late 17th and 18th century modifications), Valletta

'basso continuo' for the entire composition but also as part of the actual substance, part of the melody, as it were, of individual forms. The half-tones in the figures turn out in many instances to be no more than plain background surrounded by a deft highlight.

While Caravaggio's figures retain their old force of three-dimensionality and *rilievo* (relief), the balance between lights and darks has become more subtle. The canvases have a porosity that absorbs light with such force that the figures seem virtually imprisoned by the ambient space. Caravaggio's minimalism also extends to his range of colour – a restricted spectrum of browns and greys with a single splash of red serving as his only strong chromatic element – and to his new habit of leaving large areas of the canvas bare.

Minimal too were the number of works Caravaggio produced in this long and – until August 1608 – strangely peaceful period. This, in fact, was the longest stretch in a single locale of his post-Roman career. Given how few paintings Caravaggio is known to have created on the island, his seemingly rapid technique would appear to have little or nothing to do with time constraints.[5] His daring brushwork and new economy of means, which in certain cases test the limits of what could

Fig. 20. *View of Valletta from Vittoriosa*

be considered a finished work, are instead signs of a new confidence in his approach to painting.

Our knowledge of what Caravaggio painted on the island is based on the rather patchy evidence provided by a handful of biographies,[6] two documents,[7] and a smattering of observations penned by Seicento travellers.[8] Since it is likely that one of Caravaggio's primary motives for going to Malta was to obtain a knighthood, it follows that the artist may have donated some of his pictures to the Order. This may explain why no financial transactions for Caravaggio in Malta have been discovered.

The most important source for the 1607–08 period is unquestionably Bellori. In the *Vite de' pittori* (Rome 1672), he says Caravaggio made the following works during his Maltese sojourn: two portraits of Grand Master Alof de Wignacourt – one showing him standing dressed in armour (located, according to the author, in the Knights' Armoury) and another showing him seated without armour;[9] and three works for St John's – the *Beheading of St John the Baptist* (the Oratory is not mentioned) and two half-length paintings, a *Magdalene* and a *St Jerome Writing*, situated above the two doors of the Chapel of the Italian Langue.[10] According to Bellori, Caravaggio made a sixth picture in Malta, another *St Jerome*. This one he says is located in the palace and shows the saint with a skull, 'meditating on death'. Since the first image was a depiction of the saint 'writing', the implication is that the work in the palace had a different composition.[11] This second *Jerome* may be identical with a Riberesque work attributed to van Somer hanging today in the Grand Master's Palace.[12]

As will be demonstrated, all the pictures described by Bellori are traceable, though fully three of them (four, if the van Somer painting is in fact the biographer's *Penitent Jerome*) are almost certainly cases of mistaken identity. Bellori, it seems, never visited Malta.[13] Obvious errors of attribution in his text lead to the conclusion that he relied on a poorly informed correspondent (probably after 1661) for this section of the biography.[14]

Grand Master Alof de Wignacourt and a Page

Bellori's predecessor Baglione (1642) was the first to mention that Caravaggio had painted a portrait of the Grand Master. It so pleased the prince, Baglione writes, that he rewarded the artist with the habit of the Order.[15] The author does not describe the picture, but it is likely that he is referring to one of Caravaggio's most uncharacteristic paintings, the *Portrait of Grand Master Alof de Wignacourt and a Page*, now in the Louvre (fig. 21; pls. I–III).[16]

There are no early documents for this work, which, based on style and context (paying tribute to the Grand Master), was probably done in late 1607, soon after Caravaggio arrived on the island. The second person to cite the painting was the English traveller and diarist John Evelyn,[17] who in 1644 observed the portrait hanging in Paris in the rue de Seine palace of Roger de Plessis, duc de la Rocheguyon et de Liancourt (1598–1674), a major collector of Italian baroque pictures, who, so far as I have been able to ascertain, was neither a member of the Order of St John nor a relative of Wignacourt.[18] By 1670 the picture is recorded in the collection of Louis XIV.[19]

It is not known where the picture was kept on the island (though the Grand Master's Palace would be a prime candidate). Since no contemporary copies of the work have been identified other than an extremely mediocre derivation at the Verdala Palace that carries an

Fig. 21. *Portrait of Alof de Wignacourt and a Page,* Paris, Louvre

Fig. 22. Anonymous, *Portrait of Alof de Wignacourt,* Malta, Verdala Palace

inscription based on Wignacourt's death date of 14 September 1622 (fig. 22),[20] it is possible that Caravaggio's portrait of the Grand Master left Malta relatively early.

The Verdala picture shows the Grand Master without the page and with his arms in a different position with respect to the Louvre canvas. The work's condition is quite compromised and, thus, dating is difficult. The head appears to be completely repainted. On the left side of the composition, there are traces of a table with a helmet perched on top of it. Certain elements, such as the internal proportions of the armour, are sufficiently different from Caravaggio's painting that one suspects the artist was not working with the original canvas in front of him. He probably relied on memory or a varied copy; he may have re-posed the armour and worked from that (though certain ornaments on the suit are missing). Because of the inscription, it may be hypothesised that the work dates approximately to 1622–25. The style of the picture, moreover, with its obliviousness to Caravaggism, also suggests an artist working long after Merisi had left the island.

Elected for life to the chief position of the Order in 1601,[21] Alof de Wignacourt almost at once proved to be a great military leader. Much of his magistry was devoted to protecting the islands from attacks. But he also organised numerous military campaigns against the Turks in the Eastern Mediterranean, successfully recapturing islands that had for years been in Ottoman possession. Many engraved frontispieces bearing his likeness contain references to his victories at Patras, Lepanto, Lango, and the city of Mahomet in Barbary.[22]

Caravaggio shows the ageing Grand Master as a proud, feisty warrior with a look of sublime confidence on his face (fig. 21; pl. II). In a format based on Titian but made both more flexible and more austere,[23] he steps towards the left but turns his head towards the right, looking over his shoulder as if to inspect his troops, making sure 'these youngsters' are keeping up with him.[24] Wearing a classic suit of Milanese armour of c. 1565–80, Wignacourt holds a commander's baton with both of his gauntleted hands. The poise and glowing face of the Grand Master suggest that this scene might be no more than a moment excerpted from a drill or parade. But his firm grip on the baton, by contrast, is a poignant metaphor of his tight rule over his Order and a warning to the enemy not to test his readiness to engage.[25]

At his side, the young page (pl. III) holds the Grand Master's helmet and red-and-white surcoat while moving in the opposite direction to Wignacourt's glance. A wonderful intersection of axes is thereby created, knitting the two figures together more by action and gaze than by placement. Perhaps the best-preserved part of the picture, the page, one of twelve who served the Grand Master,[26] looks out at the viewer, making sure we recognise his good fortune in being favoured by this powerful prince.[27]

Bellori's description of a full-length portrait of Wignacourt, which he locates in the Armoury, does not mention the page, and is unlikely to be identical with the Louvre picture (which, it should be remembered, had already left the island and was seen in Paris by 1644). It corresponds instead to a *Portrait of Wignacourt* (fig. 23) formerly in the Armoury showing the Grand Master alone and *in piedi armato* (standing in armour).[28] This modest work, which is now in the National Museum of Fine Arts, Valletta, has been attributed to Leonello Spada as well as to Cassarino, though without consensus.[29] A slightly varied copy, of lesser quality, still hangs in the Ambassadors' room in the Grand Master's Palace. There are

Fig. 23. Anonymous, *Portrait of Alof de Wignacourt Standing in Armour,* Valletta, National Museum of Fine Arts

numerous other replicas and variants of the picture, which was obviously Wignacourt's official portrait in Malta.

Bellori's informant made yet another blunder, if we are right in thinking that his *seduto e disarmato* (seated without armour) portrait of the Grand Master is comparable to (or identical with) a *Portrait of Wignacourt* in the Collegio Wignacourt Museum, Rabat (fig. 24).[30] This stiff work, which follows a worn-out, late-Cinquecento formula used for earlier Grand Master portraits, carries two inscriptions, one stating Wignacourt's age as 70, and another indicating that the picture was made for Fra Louis Perrin du Bus in 1617.[31] Neither the National Museum portrait nor the Rabat canvas has even the slightest hint of Caravaggism; they are not copies of Caravaggios mentioned by Bellori that have gone missing. Given how closely they mirror the biographer's descriptions, one suspects they are the very same works Bellori's informant identified as paintings by Caravaggio.

Fig. 24. Anonymous, *Portrait of Alof de Wignacourt Seated*, Rabat, Malta, Collegio Wignacourt Museum

On the basis of style and the age of the sitter, the National Museum portrait (fig. 23) can be plausibly dated to c. 1612–15. It is particularly interesting in that it shows the Grand Master wearing an entirely different suit of armour than the one depicted by Caravaggio in the Louvre portrait. Both suits survive and are preserved in the Armoury in Valletta.

Unlike the heavy, old-fashioned harness of c. 1565–80 painted by Caravaggio (fig. 25),[32] the armour shown in the National Museum portrait, also of Milanese manufacture, is light and extremely ornate; it is obviously from the early Baroque period (fig. 26). This second suit, among the great pieces of Italian armour of the early Seicento, is traditionally dated to 1610–20.[33] The presumption has always been that Caravaggio never had the opportunity to paint the second harness, since its date of manufacture was subsequent to the artist's flight from Malta.[34]

When the two suits are seen side by side in the Armoury, it is immediately noticeable that the earlier armour (fig. 25), the one

Fig. 25. Milanese Armourer, *Armour,* c. 1565–80, Valletta, National Armoury

Fig. 26. Milanese Armourer, *Armour belonging to Alof de Wignacourt*, c. 1601–2, Valletta, National Armoury

depicted by Caravaggio, would never have fit the Grand Master, who was a shorter, thinner man. Moreover, unlike the more modern harness (fig. 26), which is covered with Wignacourt's coat of arms, the earlier suit has no marks or inscriptions that would link it to Caravaggio's patron. In all likelihood, then, the earlier suit was simply used by Caravaggio as a studio prop, which would help explain why there is a slight awkwardness in the handling of the relationship in the portrait between the head and the armour.[35]

The discovery of a series of documents forces a redating of Wignacourt's personal armour (fig. 26) and throws new light on the Grand Master as a patron, one concerned with how he would appear in public and with the quality of objects associated with his person. On 19 February 1601, a mere nine days after his election, Wignacourt sat down with his secretary to pen one of the very first letters of his magistry. This missive, directed to one of his Receivers, and the score of related dispatches that followed until the armour finally arrived on 12 August 1602, show an impatient Wignacourt obsessed with this full (and no doubt extremely expensive) suit of armour he ordered from Milan. 'We wish to be armed from head to foot', the Grand Master announces, 'and the armour should not only be of fine and perfect temper, but of showy and beautiful craftsmanship, and with all those gold embellishments that can properly be fit on it. Similarly, provide us with a weapon, such that on those occasions when one has to rush out at night in armour, we could carry the weapon in our hand. Not only must the weapon be light, noble, and strong, but if necessary it should injure. And thus, select an invention that has all the above qualities in order that it be worthy of being seen in the hands ...'[36]

This rare letter, and the several others that followed it, despite referring to a suit Caravaggio did not paint, provide invaluable insights into how Wignacourt would have instructed the artist when the portrait now in the Louvre was first contemplated. At the same time, the letters also complicate matters, since they demonstrate – contrary to generally held opinion – that the more modern armour was made in 1601 and not ten or twenty years later.[37] Consequently, it was in Wignacourt's possession long before, rather than long after, Caravaggio made this stunning effigy of his patron.

It is a mystery why Wignacourt and Caravaggio decided that the old-fashioned armour, which had belonged to another knight, would serve them better than the flashy (*vistosa*) new suit Alof had worried about for eighteen months – a suit covered with the Wignacourt family fleurs-de-lys. A proper, if still speculative, answer goes beyond the scope of this general study. No doubt the idea of alluding to the Battle of Lepanto (or even to the 1565 Siege) through a veteran's harness was part of the scheme.[38] However, I suspect stylistic issues raised by Caravaggio were also debated. Unparalleled in his ability to depict armour (most of it quite plain), Caravaggio may have balked at painting such a frilly suit. It would have taken all the drama away from this classic picture, which was greatly admired by Ingres.

Portrait of Wignacourt 'in aovato'

Caravaggio was an accomplished portraitist – since his earliest days in Milan, according to Bellori. And it is not surprising to learn that he painted Wignacourt a second time in what was probably a bust-length image in an oval format (*in aovato*) owned by the Florentine knight Fra Francesco dell'Antella (1567–1624). The picture, not mentioned by the biographers and now lost, is specifically listed as a Caravaggio in an early and highly reliable document of 1623 pertaining to the Florentine church of San Jacopo in Campo Corbolini,[39] a *commenda* given to Fra Francesco on 27 April 1611. Dell'Antella left Malta in July of that same year, soon after he killed the Grand Master's nephew (in self-defence).[40] He probably took the portrait home with him at this time.

Proud of the special relationship he had with Wignacourt, whom he served for years as Secretary of Italian letters, the Commendatore placed the image, side by side with his own oval portrait painted by Justus Sustermans (fig. 27), on the wall of the loggia facing the garden at San Jacopo.[41] I suspect Sustermans' canvas was custom-made to be a pendant to Caravaggio's. If so, the lost portrait's dimensions would have been roughly the same, 58 x 43 cm, and the sitter's glance would have been directed towards the right (thus concealing the mole on the left side of Wignacourt's nose, just as in the Louvre portrait).

Fig. 27. Justus Sustermans, *Portrait of Fra Francesco dell'Antella*, Florence, Alberto Bruschi collection

Sleeping Cupid

In 1609, some two years before the incident with Wignacourt's nephew, dell'Antella, a learned man who would soon become an official member of the Accademia del Disegno in Florence,[42] shipped an important painting from Malta to his family palace in Piazza Santa Croce. Indeed, the Commendatore treasured this little work, as we learn from a 1609 letter written in Malta by dell'Antella's friend, the Florentine knight Fra Francesco Buonarroti (1574–1632), an amateur architect and ambitious member of the Order.[43] The letter is addressed to the latter's brother, Michelangelo Buonarroti the Younger, back in Florence: 'For your information, you should know that on two or three occasions I have been in conversation with Signor Antella, who tells me that he has sent there a picture of a sleeping Cupid by the hand of Michelangelo da Caravaggio, to the house of Signor Niccolò [dell'Antella] his brother; the Commendatore regards it as a jewel (*una*

Fig. 28. *Sleeping Cupid*, Florence, Pitti Palace

gioia), and is very happy for it to be seen, so that others can express an opinion on it. And because it moved someone who saw it to compose some sonnets about it, which he has shown me, thus I imagine he would greatly value your going to see it'.[44]

The work, of course, is Caravaggio's *Sleeping Cupid* now in the Pitti Palace (fig. 28; pls. XVII–XIX), the only mythological painting Caravaggio is known to have created on the island and perhaps his last essay in this genre.[45] The picture is not mentioned by the early biographers (with the exception of Baldinucci,[46] who does not record its origins in Malta). It is worth pointing out that Caravaggio had treated this subject at least once before, in a lost work that inspired a madrigal by Gaspare Murtola published in Venice in 1604 (composed in 1603 probably on the basis of a visit to Rome in 1600). It is not known how the picture seen by Murtola relates in composition to the work painted by Caravaggio now in the Pitti.[47]

Dell'Antella's letter of 24 April 1610 to Michelangelo the Younger confirms that Buonarroti, the most famous Florentine poet and playwright of his day, actually saw and enjoyed this witty painting of the Malta period, which was no doubt inspired by his great uncle's fabled, long-lost marble of this very subject. In the closing lines of the missive, dell'Antella could not hide his collector's pride in having had his work admired by this important *letterato*, descendent of the painter of the Sistine Ceiling and friend of Cigoli, Maffeo Barberini (the future Urban VIII), and Galileo. With appropriate Baroque flattery, dell'Antella exclaims: 'Now I hold my Cupid in much higher esteem than before, since it has been praised by Your Lordship'.[48]

Legend has it that Michelangelo's *Cupid* statue was deceptively sold in Rome during the sculptor's own lifetime as a true antique.[49] Michelangelo da Caravaggio's excessively naturalistic counterfeit of an ugly baby in a sexy, *all'antica* (Venus-like) pose was surely meant as a clever challenge to his more famous namesake's ultra-classicising original.[50] Something of the old satirical Caravaggio – painter of the Berlin *Amore Vincitore* and self-styled 'Michelangelo moderno' – suddenly reappears in Malta to make a final curtain call.[51] But, of course, this was a painting he must have known was destined for dell'Antella's palace in Florence, not public display in Malta, where Caravaggio seems to have presented himself as nothing less than the most polite and pious of court artists.

The Malta canvas not only ignites a *paragone* between the two Michelangelos and their duelling theories of art (ideal versus naturalistic), but it also makes claims for the superiority of the art of painting over that of sculpture.[52] Where Michelangelo's statue could only suggest night and sleep through posture and facial expression, Caravaggio's richly coloured painting creates a tenebrist environment that is more haunting and powerful than anything associated with traditional sculpture. One would have to wait for Bernini's *Ecstasy of St. Theresa* in the Cornaro Chapel for such a concept to be challenged from within the sculpture field itself.

Caravaggio's Michelangelesque references could not fail to please Florentine viewers, and one suspects dell'Antella had a large role in choosing this subject. Some scholars have suggested that the topos of 'love sleeping' is a metaphor for the vow of chastity, one of three vows (along with poverty and obedience) taken by the Knights of Malta when they profess and receive the habit of the Order.[53] There is little question that in Malta such a reading would have been plausible, indeed obvious. But, as mentioned above, it is likely that the picture was conceived with the idea that it would be sent to the Tuscan capital – quite far from the rhetoric of the Convent at Valletta. That the picture should be a catalyst for poetry, as remarked by Fra Francesco Buonarroti, may, in fact, have been in dell'Antella's mind from the beginning. The Commendatore's family (and later dell'Antella himself) belonged to a vibrant poetry group, the Pastori Antellesi, whose membership was a virtual galaxy of Florentine intellectuals, including Michelangelo the Younger.[54]

Caravaggio's canvas shows the god of love in a coma-like sleep, stretched out on the ground or a stone slab.[55] His quiver full of arrows has become nothing more than a pillow beneath his head. Though difficult to see in photographs, his bow – once an instrument used to incite passion – has been reduced to an unstrung, impotent artifact. A lone arrow, whose patch of red on the shaft is the only bright colour in this otherwise somber picture, is held with its wounding end sheathed by the putto's left arm. All these elements speak metaphorically of love being disarmed, of passion restrained, of earthly pleasures subdued by the world of the mind and spirit.

The extreme naturalism of the figure has had some critics wondering if Caravaggio used the corpse of a child as his model. In contrast to many of the works of the final years, in which the Lombard artist seems to have relied on memory rather than actual figures posed in the studio, the child does indeed look as if he might have been based on a real person (though, in my opinion, a living one). A medical journal article puts forth the idea that the infant pictured by Merisi suffers from juvenile rheumatoid arthritis.[56]

Caravaggio's realism may also extend to the weapon pictured in the infant's left hand (pl. XIX). An armour historian has recently suggested that it appears to be a Turkish or Indo-Persian bow of the period.[57] Such a treasure might have been seized by the Knights during one of their corsairing raids against the Turks in Barbary.[58] The rendering of the bow is a bravura demonstration of Caravaggio's skill in capturing the effects of light as it strikes objects in a dark space. This is the kind of brushwork we associate more with the tightly painted early works than with the loosely executed late pictures. The gold filigree ornament to the left of the infant's left hand, which is highly illusionistic and appears to be incised and embellished with gold leaf, is actually achieved by painting over ochre pigment with shell gold highlights.[59]

Its diminutive size and connoisseur patronage undoubtedly contributing to the props and special techniques used in this work, the *Sleeping Cupid* probably dates to the second half of Caravaggio's sojourn. The Pitti canvas's dark, honeyed complexion – most visible

Fig. 29. Battistello Caracciolo, *Sleeping Cupid*, private collection

in the bloated belly of the child – seems much closer to the tonalities of the *Beheading* than to those of the Louvre *Portrait of Wignacourt* (pl. I) or the *St Jerome* (pl. IV). It should be recalled that Fra Francesco dell'Antella was involved in the negotiations to secure Caravaggio's honorary knighthood,[60] and it is possible that the *Sleeping Cupid* was given to the Florentine as a gift in thanks for his help. If true, the work would date to sometime after February 1608.

Dell'Antella's picture became well-known in Florence almost immediately. In a novel act of advertising, Giovanni da San Giovanni used it to represent *Tranquility* in his series of allegorical frescoes completed before 1620 on the façade of the very building housing Caravaggio's work – Palazzo dell'Antella. In the fresco, the putto is accompanied by a kingfisher, the attribute of *Tranquilitas* according to Ripa.[61] Merisi's *Cupid* also inspired inventive and more explicitly erotic variations amongst Caravaggisti active in Florence. Artemisia Gentileschi – soon after leaving the Tuscan capital – turned dell'Antella's *Cupid* into a *Sleeping Venus* in a work dateable to c. 1625–30 in the Barbara Piasecka Johnson Foundation, Princeton, New Jersey.[62] The Neapolitan painter Battistello Caracciolo, possibly whilst visiting Florence in 1617–18, executed this ravishing picture of a *Sleeping Cupid* now in a private collection (fig. 29).[63] Here one senses both a strong current of Caravaggio's early homoeroticism and an admiration for Orazio and Artemisia Gentileschi's refinement in draperies and sensuous colouring. Relatively faithful copies on canvas of the Pitti

Cupid are known by Orazio Fidani in a work signed and dated 1632 (Florence, private collection),[64] and by the anonymous artist who painted the controversial picture in the Clowes Fund Collection at the Indianapolis Museum of Art.[65] Maurizio Marini has proposed the latter as an original work by Caravaggio of c. 1594-95, and connected it to the Murtola madrigal of 1603 mentioned earlier.[66] The Clowes picture, however, appears to me (based on photographs) to be a somewhat prettified, Florentinizing copy of the late 1610s or 1620s of dell'Antella's painting.[67]

Portrait of a Knight (Fra Antonio Martelli?)

Florentine patronage of Caravaggio in Malta is not unique to dell'Antella. Another senior Florentine, Fra Antonio Martelli, Prior of Messina, is the likely subject of a beautiful *Portrait of a Knight*, also in the Pitti (fig. 30; pls. XX–XXI).[68] Like the *Cupid*, this work is not mentioned by the early biographers; however, its style and subject matter argue strongly for its Maltese credentials.

The knight is shown standing, in a nearly three-quarter-length format, and wearing a black monastic habit with a large white eight-pointed cross of the Order of St John on his chest. This habit was primarily the privilege of the Grand Crosses of the Order – the Grand Master, the Conventual Bailiffs, and the Capitular Bailiffs. The elderly knight represented by Caravaggio is thus immediately recognisable as an important dignitary of the Order. He is not shown in the full *manto di punta* worn by knights at special ceremonies. These long capes, as their Italian name implies, have sleeves that end in a point (for an example, see fig. 18). Instead, Caravaggio depicts him more informally, wearing his everyday habit, with a white long-sleeve shirt underneath.

Looking solemnly towards the right side of the picture, and thus avoiding eye-contact with the spectator, the knight holds a rosary in his right hand and touches the hilt of his sword with his left (a small ring adorns his thumb). As several scholars have noted, the objects allude to the central duality of the *Sacra Religione*, an order of professed Catholic brothers who are also warriors.[69] Caravaggio sets up the two gestures with the same care and intelligence that he had used in depicting the Grand Master's hands in the *Portrait of Alof de*

Fig. 30. *Portrait of a Knight (Fra Antonio Martelli?)*, Florence, Pitti Palace

Wignacourt and a Page (fig. 21). The right hand is shown with the palm down; the left hand is shown palm up. The diagonal generated by the placement of the two hands animates the composition; it is mirrored subtly by the diagonal of the collar and the slightly downward tilt of the head.

If the Louvre *Wignacourt* is likely Caravaggio's first work on the island, the *Portrait of a Knight* is probably one of his last. The monochromatic character of this canvas and its loose, unfinished-looking brushstrokes,[70] which barely cover the reddish ground, anticipate more than any of the other works associated with the

Malta period a new chapter in Caravaggio's development. Here we see the kind of abstraction – where the brushstrokes are beginning to detach themselves from descriptive functions – that is the hallmark of pictures done in Sicily and the second Naples period. A comparison with the heads of the older male figures in the *Burial of Saint Lucy* (fig. 17) and the *Raising of Lazarus* (fig. 36) is instructive in this regard.

The Knight's right hand in particular has little colour other than that of the ground itself. The same can be said for many areas of the face. What appears as brown areas of modelling 'over' the collar and cross is a wonderful illusion: these are simply places where the priming has been allowed to show through. Such elements are part of Caravaggio's late Maltese style and not signs that the artist failed to complete the picture. Caravaggio's loose treatment of the silk cross, which bends and almost 'breathes' with the movement of the chest supporting it, is a *tour de force* that anticipates the greatest passages of Frans Hals and Velázquez.

Conservators have detected several *pentimenti* in the canvas. Most significantly, a curtain was originally painted in the upper right. Caravaggio eliminated it in the final version. Radiographs also reveal that the position of the left hand was initially lower and may have held a cross instead of a sword.[71]

It was not until 1966, when Mina Gregori identified the painting as an autograph work by Caravaggio, that the *Portrait of a Knight* re-emerged from centuries of obscurity.[72] However, the identity of the sitter himself has remained elusive. Gregori has several times suggested that the Pitti portrait depicts Grand Master Alof de Wignacourt, a view she no longer embraces.[73] In 1980, Ferdinando Bologna brought attention to a nineteenth-century print of the painting: the inscription implausibly claims that the sitter represents Fra Niccolò Caracciolo di San Vito who died in 1689.[74] Almost a decade later, Marco Chiarini published early inventory records (1666–70) describing a picture at Palazzo Pitti of similar dimensions to the canvas under consideration as a portrait of 'March'Antonio Martelli con croce di Malta' ('Fra Marc'Antonio Martelli' in an inventory of 1696).[75] Based on the suggestion of Ludovica Sebregondi, Chiarini put forward the idea that the painting might depict the Prior of Messina, Antonio Martelli, since no 'Marc'Antonio Martelli' is listed in the rolls of the Order. More recently, Gash and Sciberras have brought to light numerous archival records demonstrating that Martelli resided in Malta during Caravaggio's sojourn on the island.[76]

A member of the distinguished Florentine Martelli family, Fra Antonio di Pandolfo Martelli was born on 18 April 1534 and joined the Order of St John in 1558. As outlined in the previous chapter, he had a long and exemplary military and administrative career, which in addition to Malta also included long service in Florence and Livorno. After several years in Malta (1603–08), Martelli travelled to Messina as its new Prior,[77] arriving there on 1st November 1608.[78] Martelli's residence overlapped with the defrocked Caravaggio's stay at Messina in 1609.[79] However, it would be risky to hypothesise that Martelli comissioned the portrait in Sicily. It is hard to imagine that a major official of the Order such as Martelli would want the Convent to find out that he was patronising a man who had been cast out of the Holy Religion 'like a rotten and fetid limb' for fleeing the island without a licence.

Fra Antonio returned to his native Florence in late September 1609, and it is likely he took the Pitti portrait home with him at this time. Clearly a man with a strong constitution, he died only on 6 February 1619 at Pisa at the age of eighty-five.[80]

Caravaggio's *Portrait of a Knight* is one of a handful of images of the sixteenth and seventeenth centuries that convey the sense of service, toughness and aristocratic privilege that prevailed in the culture of the Knights of Malta. The *cavaliere* appears as a weary but nonetheless resolute old warrior – the kind of man who made the Order function even during times of diplomatic and military upheaval. Martelli (assuming it is him) clearly had suffered for the Order on more than one occasion. But despite his advanced age (he was 74 or 75 years old in 1608), he stands firm in the painting, presenting himself as a person of great ability. Caravaggio could not have failed to be impressed by such an intensely proud and accomplished individual. The intimacy of this work suggests that the Lombard artist observed Martelli on many occasions before painting this picture, with its compelling combination of movement and *gravitas*.

What we see in the Pitti *Portrait of a Knight* corresponds to an eye-witness account of Martelli's appearance only months after Caravaggio is thought to have painted the picture. A letter in the Medici Archive recently published by Fabbri, written on 2 November 1608 by Cosimo del Sera, a Medici agent at Messina, to Lorenzo Usimbardi, the granducal secretary, reports: 'Yesterday the galleys arrived here from Malta and with them Prior Martelli, who if much aged remains in excellent health'.[81]

Saint Jerome Writing

One further work of private patronage is recorded for Caravaggio in Malta. As mentioned earlier, a *St Jerome Writing* (fig. 31; pls. IV–VII)[82] is described by Bellori as hanging above the passageway in the Chapel of the Italian Langue in the Conventual Church. Indeed, for much of its history, the canvas hung in this exact position (fig. 13) before being moved, in the 1960s, to the Museum of St John's. The picture was recently placed in the Oratory of San Giovanni Decollato.[83] Bellori was also told that a *Magdalene* situated above the other doorway of the Chapel was by Caravaggio. It is almost certain that this second work is identical with a competent late sixteenth-century copy after Correggio still in the chapel, a canvas Caravaggio did not execute.[84]

First attributed in modern times to Caravaggio by Vincenzo Bonello,[85] the *St Jerome Writing* was restored by the Istituto Centrale di Restauro in Rome in 1956.[86] However, it was badly damaged when it was stolen from St John's Museum on 29 December 1985.[87] After being recovered in August 1987, it was again restored by ICR. The tension on the canvas, even after relining, is somewhat compromised because the picture had been cut out of its frame, leaving behind those areas of the canvas covering the sides of the stretcher.[88]

A miracle of wrinkles, grey hair and loose skin that would have pleased the young Rembrandt, Caravaggio's Jerome seems to be speaking the words as he writes them. Secluded in his cell-like room, cardinal's hat hung on the wall, the saint – one of the Fathers of the Latin Church – sits on the edge of the bed with his right leg positioned towards the left side of the composition. In a beautiful *contrapposto*, his head and torso are both turned in the opposite direction, towards the right. The torsion is a metaphor of the spiritual current suddenly pulsing through the saint's body as he begins to compose.

The design of the figure – basically a large triangle whose focal point is Jerome's writing hand – is given energy by the intense contrast between the reds, whites, greys, and flesh tones that make up the centre of the picture, and also by the complex outline and interior movement of the draperies. The craggy topography of the saint's anatomy and face is brought into high relief by the strong light entering the room from the upper left. Jerome's concentration is so great that he fails to notice that with his sudden turning, his garment has fallen off his shoulders and nearly landed in the pot of ink in his left hand. The patch of red drapery covering his forearm acts as a foil for the pen and hands, adding drama to the whole.

The triangular design of the body, which is cut dramatically in half by a black shadow running diagonally across the chest like a sash, is framed by the strong verticals and horizontals established by the wooden post (or door) and the rustic-looking table. Such rigorous geometry (though fashioned out of elements that are themselves somewhat flexible) is a central feature of Caravaggio's Maltese style. One does not normally think of the Lombard naturalist in terms of circles (the cardinal's hat), triangles, and rectangles, but this is precisely the language of composition he employs here.

In a strong light it is possible to see that the background area, now substantially abraded, originally contained more description of the interior of the room. A well-preserved contemporary copy of the picture (private collection) may reflect these now nearly invisible elements, including a scarf beneath the cardinal's hat.[89] The copy, whose faithfulness to the original is difficult to gauge, shows an arched opening at the extreme left, with the corner of a wall positioned just to the left of the saint's head. Thus, it would not be wrong to hypothesise that the imaginative use of deep space and architectural scenography displayed by Caravaggio in the *Beheading,* which was probably begun a few months later and completed around July 1608, is anticipated here, in a more restrained manner, in the *Jerome,* which can be dated to the end of 1607 (or the first months of 1608).

It is not known why Caravaggio painted this subject or for what location the canvas was originally intended. There is relative certainty, however, on the question of the picture's patron, thanks to the coat of arms painted prominently in the lower right corner of the canvas (fig. 12). The arms belong to one of the most important members of the Order of St John, Fra Ippolito Malaspina, Marchese di Fosdinovo and Prior of Naples (1544–1624).[90]

As discussed in detail in the previous chapter, Malaspina probably travelled to Malta on the very same galleys as Caravaggio in July

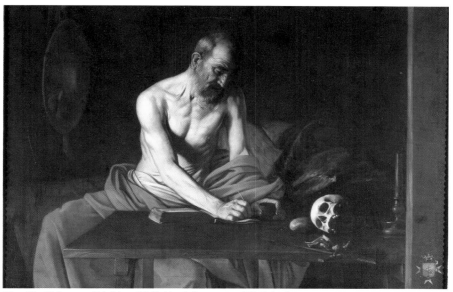

Fig. 31. *St Jerome Writing*, Valletta, Museum of St John's

1607. He was related to one of the artist's most important Roman patrons, the Genoese banker Ottavio Costa, and was, therefore, probably familiar with the artist's work before their journey to the island. Both of Costa's sons (Malaspina's great nephews) were Knights. It is possible that one of them, Alessandro, who served as one of the Grand Master's pages in this period, is the young boy pictured in Caravaggio's Louvre portrait (fig. 21).[91] Fra Ippolito was one of Wignacourt's closest allies. It was noneother than the Marchese who had single-handedly engineered Wignacourt's election as Grand Master in 1601.[92] Malaspina is buried at St John's in the Chapel of the Langue of Italy, a Langue he once presided over as *pilier*.

Indeed, it was to this Chapel, as a document of 1629 shows,[93] that Malaspina, who died five years earlier in 1624, had left an important group of paintings. This group almost certainly included Caravaggio's *St Jerome,* the *Magdalene,* and two other works which have recently been identified as part of the Prior of Naples' donation to the Chapel.[94] The confusion of Bellori's informant in thinking that Caravaggio had painted the *Magdalene* opposite the *Jerome* was probably fostered by the fact that in addition to their similarity in size and symmetrical hanging, both works carry the arms of Malaspina. The treatment of perspective in the *St Jerome,* which works best when hung at eye level (as it currently is), speaks against the commonly held notion that the picture was made for the Chapel of Italy, even though it hung there for centuries, from as early as 1629, perhaps even slightly earlier.[95]

Jerome was famous for his translations and controversial commentaries on the Bible, and spent much of his life as an outsider. A fugitive from Rome and no stranger to accusations of blasphemy himself, Caravaggio seems to have related to the ascetic, meditative saint. This is a particularly lonely looking Jerome compared to most. The barreness of his cell, the worn quality of his hat, the poverty conveyed by the still life elements (some of the finest passages of painting of Caravaggio's final years) make this an exceptionally inward-looking, reflective picture. The classical restraint, limited chromatic range, and subtle body language of the *Jerome* would be put to good use in another picture he began for the knights around this time.

The Beheading of St John

Arguably the masterpiece of his career and one of the most gripping images in all of Baroque art, the *Beheading of Saint John the Baptist* (pls. VIII–XVI) is Michelangelo da Caravaggio's largest painting[96] and the only extant work by him that bears his signature.[97] The letters 'f. MichelAn . . .' are formed out of the blood spewing from the freshly cut neck of the Baptist.

Painted as the altarpiece for the Oratory of San Giovanni Decollato, the recently restored picture[98] was probably started soon after March 1608, that is, after Caravaggio learned that the Pope had sent a waiver to make him a knight. It has been suggested that the work was given to the Order in lieu of a proper *passaggio*, the gift – usually money – knights presented to the Religione upon being admitted as a member.[99] Because the signature, 'f[ra] Michelan[gelo]', makes reference to Caravaggio's new status as a knight (his installation was on 14 July 1608), the canvas must have been completed after that date. It is likely that it was unveiled on 29 August, the feast of St John's Decollation, the Oratory's titular.[100]

The function of the Oratory and its architectural, pictorial and sculptural development over the course of the seventeenth century have been the focus of two recent studies, so only brief mention needs be made here.[101] Before Mattia Preti (another Italian artist who became a Knight of Malta) turned the hall into a Baroque spectacle in the 1680s, the room was quite simple, giving much greater force and resonance to the taut design of Caravaggio's painting, which would have dominated the space much more than it presently does.

An engraving of 1650 representing the knights' tribunal or Sguardio, which regularly met in the Oratory, gives a general idea of what the hall looked like before Preti's intervention (fig. 18).[102] Built in 1602–05 over the cemetery where knights, including those martyred by the Turks, were interred, the Oratory owes its origins to a petition from several knights who wanted to move their Confraternity of the Misericordia to St John's. This organisation, like its more famous counterpart of San Giovanni Decollato in Rome, accompanied prisoners to the gallows. Caravaggio was no doubt familiar with the traditions of this Roman brotherhood and the imposing paintings of the *Beheading* by Giorgio Vasari and Roviale Spagnuolo (attrib.) in its church and oratory respectively. In addition to hosting elections, installation ceremonies, tribunals, and defrockings, the Knights' Oratory was also used for the training and devotions of the novices, who had their own special commissioners and theologian.

Although the Oratory, the showplace of his defrocking, has come to symbolise Caravaggio's defeat – his difficulty in controlling his violent temper – the *Beheading* by contrast stands as a memorial to how brilliantly he controlled violence in his art. Nowhere has an artist better balanced extremes of emotion and savagery with order and stillness. Discipline of a classical nature is everywhere apparent in the *Beheading*, whose setting is an austere prison courtyard, unyielding in its geometry, cold and unfeeling in its stony surfaces.[103]

Nicely described by Bellori,[104] who noted that the artist had put everything he had into this work (*usò ogni potere del suo pennello*),[105] Caravaggio's *Beheading* is a theatre of voids, displacements, and arrested actions. It is easy to kill a man, but the world remains permanently askew as a result.

The drama takes place wholly on the left side of the composition (fig. 32), where a human arch of four figures, mocked by the titanic architecture behind it, presides over the slaughter of John, the Holy Precursor, who is placed flat on the floor like a sacrificial lamb. Caravaggio situates the woolly hooves of John's garment stategically near the saint's head to reinforce this idea of the Baptist's martyrdom paving the way for Christ's own sacrifice on the cross.[106] The executioner, whom Herod has appointed to cut off the Baptist's head, is terrifying in the way he stands astride his prey, grasping John's hair so that he can gain better access to the neck. He steps on a strip of John's blood-red drapery, a seemingly arbitrary act that reinforces the realism of the scene.

The brute has already killed John with his sword, but now reaches back for a small knife, the *misericordia*,[107] to cleave the head from the body (pl. XV). Dressed in a dark turquoise (not Turkish)[108] jacket and weighed down by a set of huge keys, the jailer points impassively to the basin as if to hurry the executioner along (pls. XIII–XIV). Yet the narrative remains frustratingly incomplete: Caravaggio's composition is so utterly static that we know the knife will never fully emerge from its sheath. Time and action are forever frozen in this picture whose starkness and simplicity recall the great murals of Giotto and Masaccio.

The girl (pl. XI), whose common clothes and apron define her as a servant rather than Salome (Bellori calls her Herodias),[109] stands ready with her golden basin to receive the human trophy, the product of a rash oath taken by Herod. But her timing is not synchronised with the movements of the executioner; indeed, her arms seem to grow longer as she, like the audience to Caravaggio's drama, must remain patient.

The huge rectangle framing the low prison window[110] challenges the quoined arch at left for prominence. Two forlorn prisoners (pl. XVI) watch with quiet sadness. They have seen this act from their front-row seats many times before. Perhaps they know this is a rehearsal for their own punishment.

Only one figure in this picture is demonstrably horrified by what she witnesses. The old woman (pl. XII), perhaps a companion to the girl or a prison nurse, uniquely displays the signs of compassion and grief such a scene should elicit. With her closed eyes and stopped ears, she reaffirms our inability to prevent this atrocity, to change the course of divinely ordered history. Her single gesture of humanity is nearly lost in the dead

Fig. 32. *Beheading of St John the Baptist*, Valletta, Oratory of San Giovanni Decollato

calm of the picture's cavernous spaces, which absorb all emotion, all action. She cannot hear that John's screams have ceased. In the interminable seconds dividing sword from knife, death and dismemberment, silence itself has been silenced.

The Annunciation

Given the inclusion of the 'f[ra]' in the signature, the date of Caravaggio's installation, and his imprisonment a month later, the *Beheading* was probably his final large work in Malta. But a powerfully composed altarpiece of the *Annunciation*, formerly in Nancy's primatial church (dedicated to Notre Dame de l'Annonciation) and now in that city's Musée des Beaux-Arts, may be a product of the last months of the Maltese period, as several scholars have suggested (pl. XXII).[111] As noted in the previous chapter, members of the Lorraine family were in Malta during Caravaggio's stay; they could have been patrons of the canvas, perhaps even the conduit for its transport to Nancy.[112]

Fig. 33. *Annunciation*, Nancy, Musée des Beaux-Arts, detail

The picture's poor state of conservation hampers stylistic analysis and the quest for a secure dating.[113] Damaged early on, the canvas has severe losses and abrasions, though the basic composition remains intact. The best-preserved passages are the shoulder and right arm of the angel and a few folds in the white drapery over the thigh (fig. 33). Only in the latter can one appreciate the range of whites, greys, and ash blacks that Caravaggio used to shape and model the forms. Despite damage, the underlying brushwork and design of the angel's drapery are stunning. The poor state of preservation of the face of the Madonna gives a false impression of what the Lombard painter intended; there is a large hole in the area of the cheek that has been repaired.

There are solid points of comparison between the *Annunciation* and the securely attributed works of Caravaggio's Maltese sojourn. The treatment of the furniture recalls elements of the *St Jerome* – especially the chair, which has the raw classical geometry and rustic texture of the table and beam in the Malaspina canvas. The picture's overall design, taut yet graceful, emphasises the exact middle of the canvas through a horizontal axis created by the right leg of the angel, the head of the Virgin, and the mattress of the bed. It is but a more compact and somewhat more elastic expression of the spartan aesthetic found in the *Beheading*. The steep diagonal that flows from upper left – across the horizontal – to lower right, electro-charged along the way by the angel's gesture as it penetrates the void above Mary's head, conveys the meaning of the story all by itself.

The Nancy altarpiece, much like the *Beheading*, is given a nearly deserted, stage-like space in the foreground. Nothing but Mary's sewing basket – the still-life equivalent of the Baptist's severed head in the Oratory canvas – establishes the picture plane and a sense of scale. The basket is treated with such psychological force that it has become a third character in this drama. I suspect it alludes, proleptically, to the crib of the Christ Child at the Nativity.

The Virgin's mantle is coloured with a blue-green pigment rarely seen in Caravaggio's oeuvre. The best comparison is the costume of the jailor in the *Beheading*, though the colours are not identical (and one must keep in mind the poor condition of the Nancy picture).[114] The lower sweep of the angel's drapery, which falls forward of the knee, seems to echo the serving girl's apron in the Oratory canvas, which may have been painted just weeks before. It is the *disegno* of the girl's overly long arm and exposed elbow in the *Beheading* that seems most obviously reborn in the annunciate angel, whose head similarly is pushed up against the right shoulder.

If the *Annunciation* is a Malta picture, as its patronage and style seem to suggest, it joins the *St Jerome* and the *Beheading* as testaments to the creative strides made by Caravaggio during his fifteen months on the island. It would also moot a frequently debated observation that Caravaggio made surprisingly few works during his relatively long service to the knights.

This distinguished service (before a fatal error in judgement brought it to a sudden halt) did not go unnoticed by the person who had championed the artist and proclaimed him the Apelles of Malta. According to Bellori, in recompense for the *Beheading*, Grand Master Wignacourt put a rich gold chain around Caravaggio's neck and awarded him two slaves.[115] An engraving in Bellori's book (see frontispiece, above) shows Caravaggio as a proud *cavaliere*.[116] He wears the black-and-white habit of the Order – clearly recognisable by the white eight-pointed cross embroidered across the breast

– and holds a sword, a key attribute for a knight. Poking up from the folds of drapery over his chest, a second Maltese cross, this one probably made of gold, hangs from a chain (no doubt an allusion to Wignacourt's gift). Though Bellori obviously knew a fair amount about Caravaggio's misfortunes in Malta, the fact that he had him depicted in 1672 as a Knight of St John suggests that he may have been unaware that the artist had been defrocked in December 1608. Or perhaps Bellori was being charitable, in a biography quick to point out artistic and human shortcomings, in portraying Fra Michelangelo da Caravaggio in his moment of greatest achievement.

NOTES

I am extremely grateful to the American Academy in Rome, the Metropolitan Museum of Art, the Institute for Advanced Study, the Andrew W. Mellon Foundation, and the University of Delaware for their generous support of my research on Caravaggio and the Knights of Malta.

1. This essay is much indebted to overviews of the period in Hibbard 1983; Cutajar 1989; Gash 1993; Puglisi 1998; Gregori, in Florence 1999; Langdon 1999; Spike 2001; Marini 2001; and many other studies. For bibliography, see Cinotti 1983; for more recent publications, see Spike 2001 (CD-Rom).
2. For the earlier history of painting in Malta, see Buhagiar 1987; and Gash 1993. For Paladini in Malta, see most recently Stone 1997[2]; and Sciberras–Stone 2001.
3. For the palace see Ganado 2001. For the church see Scicluna 1955; and Cutajar 1999.
4. On the early history of the Oratory, see Stone 1997[1].
5. Several scholars have speculated that Caravaggio made one or more trips to Naples in 1607–8, and that such absences from Malta account for the small number of works he made on the island. However, if one includes the large altarpiece of the *Annunciation* as a Malta painting (see below), the quantity of pictures becomes more reasonable for a 15-month period. We should consider that during his sojourn, Caravaggio was probably also participating in some of the religious and military exercises normally required of novices. There is no documentary or circumstantial evidence that Caravaggio left the island before his escape from prison in fall 1608. Moreover, so far as we know, Caravaggio had no dispensation for an 'abito fuori convento'; he could not simply come and go as he pleased, but had to stay on the island ('in convento') to fulfill his one-year novitiate as required by the Knights' statutes. There are no works associated with Naples that in my opinion have the stamp of the 'Maltese' style.
6. G. Mancini (ms. of c. 1617–21) simply says that he made 'alcune opere con gusto del Gran Maestro' (Hibbard 1983, p. 348). G. Baglione, *Vite de' pittori*, Rome 1642, is not much more helpful, naming only the portrait of Wignacourt: 'Poscia andossene a Malta, & introdotto a far riverenza al gran Maestro, fecegli il ritratto; onde quel Principe in segno di merito, dell'habito di s. Giovanni il regalò, e creallo Cavaliere di gratia' (Hibbard 1983, p. 355). F. Scannelli (*Il Microcosmo della pittura*, Cesena 1657) does not mention the Malta episode. G.P. Bellori (1672), who wrote the most detailed life of Caravaggio, is discussed below. L. Scaramuccia (*Le finezze de' pennelli italiani*, Pavia 1674) refers only to Caravaggio's 'passaggio à Malta' (Hibbard 1983, p. 374). C.C. Malvasia (*Felsina Pittrice*, Bologna, 1678; ed. cit 1841, II, p. 76), mentions Caravaggio's visit to Malta when recounting (with some

invenzione) Leonello Spada's trip to the island. He seems to refer obliquely to Caravaggio's portrait of Wignacourt when he writes of Spada parading arrogantly through Bologna upon his return from Malta, with a sword on his belt – 'e collana al collo, che dicea donatagli da quel gran mastro per avergli fatto anch'egli il ritratto'. On Spada's trip to Malta, see Sciberras–Stone 2001, p. 144. J. von Sandrart, in his *Academie der Bau-, Bild-, und Mahlery-Künste von 1675* (Nuremberg 1675) states that 'he painted the Beheading of St. John the Baptist in the church at Malta, which is marvelous because of its truth to nature, as well as some other paintings' (trans. Hibbard 1983, p. 379). On Sandrart's visit to Malta, see Freller 2002. Baldinucci 1681–1728 (ed. 1846), III, p. 686, mentions the two portraits of Wignacourt and the *Beheading*; his text generally follows Bellori's narrative. Similiarly, F. Susinno, *Vite de' pittori messinesi* (ms. dated 1724), records the same three works, but is more specific when it comes to the two portraits of the Grand Master: one 'in pie' armato' and the other 'vestito in abito signorile di pompa' (see Hibbard 1983, pp. 380–1).

7. See Sebregondi Fiorentini 1982; and Stone 1997[2]. See below.
8. Balsamo 1996; and Stone 1997[1], p. 164, n. 22.
9. 'Era il Caravaggio desideroso di ricevere la croce di Malta, solita darsi per grazia ad uomini riguardevoli per merito e per virtù; fece però risoluzione di trasferirsi in quell'isola, dove giunto fu introdotto avanti il Gran Maestro Vignacourt, signore francese. Lo ritrasse in piedi armato ed a sedere disarmato nell'abito di Gran Maestro, conservandosi il primo ritratto nell'armeria di Malta' (Bellori, in Hibbard 1983, p. 368).
10. 'Per la Chiesa medesima di San Giovanni, entro la cappella della nazione Italiana dipinse due mezze figure sopra due porte, la Madalena e San Girolamo che scrive' (Bellori, in Hibbard 1983, p. 369).
11. 'Fece un altro San Girolamo con un teschio nella meditazione della morte, il quale tuttavia resta nel palazzo' (Bellori, in Hibbard 1983, p. 369).
12. Sciberras–Stone 2005[2], p. 12, and fig. 8. As R. Spear recently pointed out to me, the Van Somer is a copy after Ribera's *St Jerome* of c. 1640–2 in the Cleveland Museum of Art (Spear 1971, cat. no. 57, illus., who also mentions the Malta picture, though without attribution).
13. Hibbard 1983, pp. 235, 327, is incorrect in stating that the biographer travelled to the island. Cinotti 1983, p. 487, remarks that Bellori was in Naples in 1661.
14. See Sciberras–Stone 2005[2], pp. 11–12; and see below.
15. Hibbard 1983, p. 355, and see note 6 above. Bellori repeats the same information in relation to the two portraits he describes: 'Laonde questo signore gli donò in premio la croce' (Bellori, in Hibbard 1983, p. 368).
16. The 195 x 134 cm canvas, already in poor condition in the eighteenth century, is quite compromised and in need of restoration. For this reason it could not be loaned to the Naples-London exhibition. The painting's condition and the fact that, as an official portrait, this is an unusual subject for the master, have no doubt weighed in the deliberations of those scholars who question the attribution. However, today, nearly all experts assign the work to Caravaggio. (For those few who continue to raise doubts, it should be borne in mind that no painter exhibiting this quality of invention and execution – other than Caravaggio – is known to have been resident in Malta during the period when, judging from Wignacourt's age in the picture, this work was made.) The present author has recently completed a broad study of this portrait, with special attention to the culture and politics of the pages of the Order. See Stone, 'The Apelles of Malta: Caravaggio and his Grand Master', forthcoming.
17. Cinotti 1983, p. 489.
18. For the Conte de Liancourt as a collector (including Evelyn's visit), see Schnapper 1994, pp. 159–64. He owned such masterpieces as the *Diana as Huntress* by Orazio Gentileschi, now in Nantes.
19. For provenance and bibliography, see Cinotti 1983, pp. 487–9.
20. Inv. 5815. 195 x 134.5 cm. The Verdala Palace portrait is cited by Marini 2001, p. 539, as being in Santa Maria della Vittoria in Valletta. However, some years ago it was transferred.
21. Born in Picardy in 1547, he took the habit on 25 August 1566. See Galea 2002.
22. For various engraved portraits of Wignacourt, see Gregori 1974.
23. See Puglisi 1998, p. 293, for Venetian and Lombard sources for the work.
24. Caravaggio's idea of posing the Grand Master looking over his left shoulder was probably

25. While the left hand holds the baton with the palm down and would seem to be the hand to actually use the weapon, the right hand is held palm up so the baton can be quickly released. Gregori, in *Age of Caravaggio* 1985, p. 330, notes the unusualness of this gesture: 'This detail underscores Caravaggio's independence toward traditional iconographic conventions and probably accounts for the presence of pentimenti in this part of the picture'. The pilgrim in the *Seven Works* (fig. 6) holds his staff in a similar gesture, as C. Puglisi recently suggested to me.

26. The maximum number used to be eight, but in the Chapter General of 1603 a.i. [1604], it was raised to twelve.

27. It has been suggested by several scholars that the young boy is Alessandro Costa, Ottavio Costa's son. See Spike 2001, p. 206, and nn. 682–3, with previous bibliography. For Costa's nomination as a page, see Macioce 1994, p. 227. In 1608, he would have been eleven years old. The identification of the page as Costa is a possibility, but is undocumented. There are at least eleven other contenders for the sitter. On Costa, see now also Sciberras–Stone 2005², n. 41.

28. Inv. 199. 232 x 152 cm. Restored in 1987–8.

29. The National Museum picture, in my opinion, shows no trace of Leonello Spada's hand. I have consulted with several of my fellow Bolognese painting specialists, including Emilio Negro (who recently saw the painting in Malta) and Daniele Benati, who agree with this view.

30. 136 x 113 cm.; Azzopardi 1990, cat. no. 1, illus. on p. 265 (entry by A. Espinosa). In the same Collegio is another portrait of Wignacourt 'seduto e disarmato', probably painted around the same time (200 x 135 cm; cat. no. 58; ill. on p. 404; entry by Espinosa on p. 405; inscribed with the Grand Master's death date of 1622).

31. A third inscription on the canvas, the famous G.NF.D.C. monogram, awaits further study. The *Ruolo Generale* (1886) at NLM gives the date of admission of Fra Louis Le Parain, known as de Bus, as 25 December 1602.

32. Laking 1903, no. 139, pl. XI (as School of Lucio Picinino, Milan, c. 1580).

33. Laking 1903, no. 413, pl. XXV (as Milanese, probably by Geronimo Spacini, c. 1610–20). I thank Donald J. LaRocca and Stuart W. Pyhrr of the Department of European Arms and Armor, Metropolitan Museum of Art, New York, for discussing these two pieces of armour with me. Further technical details are examined in Stone 'Apelles'.

34. The earliest study of the Louvre painting, by Maindron 1908, is mostly concerned with the two suits of armour discussed here. More recently, Rossi 2000, pp. 84–5, suggested that the second suit of armour was a gift from the pope to Wignacourt, and that this gift did not arrive until 1608, after Caravaggio had been forced to use the old-fashioned suit of armour as a substitute. However, as new documents show (see below), the situation was quite different. No documents substantiate the idea that the pope sent Wignacourt a suit of armour in 1608.

35. It is doubtful that Caravaggio cajoled the Grand Master into modelling this armour for him – and, as just mentioned, it probably did not fit. Typical studio practice would begin with a simple sitting in which the painter worked out the position and form of the head and the basic pose of the body. Only later would the tedious rendering of the armour – perhaps modelled by an assistant – be done. Caravaggio's 'del naturale' methods perhaps got the better of him here, because the proportions he so faithfully rendered in each of the two elements do not quite go together. The earlier suit of armour was used as a studio prop many times. For example, it appears in an anonymous, mid-17th-century portrait of *Fra Jean-Jacques de Verdelain* (Valletta, National Armoury); see Cardini 2004, cat. no. 23. Parts of the suit are also featured in a well-known portrait of *Grand Master Manuel Pinto de Fonseca* by Pierre Bernard of c. 1741–3 (Valletta, Grand Master's Palace); see Degiorgio–Fiorentino 2004, pp. 29–30.

36. Translation author. AOM, Arch. 1380 (1601), f. 50*v*: 'Quartieri a 19 di Febbraio [in Milan, 1601]. Sendo noi consapevoli . . . della prattica che avete in Milano, dove si fanno bellissime e buonissime armature, abbiamo pensato servirci dell'opera vostra,

e però vi commettiamo che in sù le misure che vi saran mandate da Genova dal nostro Procurator Torreglia ci facciate fabricare una armatura per la nostra persona, che ci armi dal capo fino a' piedi, la quale desideriamo non solo sia de' fine, e perfetta tempra [tempera], ma di vistosa e bella mastria, con tutti quelli adornamenti di oro, et alora che vi si possino con proporzione accomodare, e parimente ci provediate d'un arme che in occasione d'aver a uscire fuora quando di notte si desse all'arme possiamo portarla in mano, che non solo deve esser leggiera, nobile e forte, ma che possa bisognando offendere, che però piglierete qualche inventione che abbia tutte le sopradette qualità in modo che sia degnia d'esser vista nelle mani . . . 'For the armour's arrival, see AOM Arch. 1381 (1602), ff. 204 *r–v*. The present author discovered these documents and presented them in public lectures at Columbia and Emory universities in 1999. For a more complete treatment, with full transcriptions, see Stone 'Apelles'.

37. For an excellent discussion of the armour and the development of the Malta Armoury, see Spiteri 2003, pp. 229–38, who recently also found the documents.

38. Calvesi 1990, pp. 364–5.

39. Sebregondi Fiorentini 1982, pp. 108, 117, and nn. 15–16. See now also Sebregondi 2005, pp. L–LI. 'Per il ritratto del Gran Maestro Vignacourt in aovato col suo adornamento d'oro affisso nel muro in testa della loggia che entra nell'orto, di mano del Caravaggio, a perpetua [. . .] Memoria della Gratitudine che conserva a detto Gran Maestro il suddetto Signor Commendatore, per havergli donato di gratia la suddetta commenda di Santo Jacopo in Campo Corbolini; et al riscontro di detto ritratto del Gran Maestro il detto Commendatore vi ha affisso il suo proprio'. ASF (Archivio di Stato, Florence), CRSGF 132, Filza 112, *Scritture diverse della Commenda di San Jacopo in Campo Corbolini posseduta dal Sig.r Com.re Antella dell'anno 1621*. The document is a list of expenditures (including those of prior years) registered between February and April 1623 (1622 a.i.).

40. Stone 1997[2], pp. 171–2, with docs.

41. I thank Ludovica Sebregondi for an enlightening tour of the church and commandery palace. After years of neglect, the church is currently being restored with her expert guidance. For the Sustermans portrait, see her entry in Venice 2000, cat. no. 35, p. 163. Another portrait of dell'Antella, this one full length and made in 1618 when the Commendatore was 51 years old (as inscribed on the picture), has also been attributed to Sustermans. Recently, this work has been ascribed to the workshop of the Casini; see Gregori 2000, fig. 10 (ill. in colour). For the history of the church, see now Sebregondi *San Jacopo*.

42. He is the designer of the magnificent bird's-eye view of Valletta illustrated above (fig. 9). For dell'Antella as a map-maker, see Ganado 2003, pp. 330–42.

43. For Francesco Buonarroti, see Sebregondi Fiorentini 1986; and Stone 1997[2]. Fra Francesco had prints after Michelangelo with him on the island. He may also have had original drawings by the sculptor with him as well. He also brought to Malta one of the earliest copies of the *Vocabolario della Crusca*, the most important Italian dictionary of its kind.

44. Translation author. 'Per Vostra intelligenza sappiate che mi son trovato dua o tre volte in ragionamento con il Signor Antella, il quale mi dice haver mandato costà un quadro di mano di Michelangelo da Caravaggio, dentrovi un Cupido che dorme, in casa il Signor Niccolò suo fratello, il quale il Signor Commendatore lo tiene per una gioia, e ha gran piacere che sia visto perché gli sia detto l'opinione altrui e perché qualchuno che l'ha visto ci ha composto sopra qualche sonetto, i quali esso mi ha mostri, perciò m'immagino ch'esso avrebbe caro lo vedessi' (as transcribed in Sebregondi 2005, p. XLV). ABF (Archivio Buonarroti, Casa Buonarroti, Florence) Filza 104, f. 145*r*; Sebregondi Fiorentini 1982, p. 122, first published the document.

45. 71 x 105 cm. The picture has an old inscription on the reverse: 'OPERA DEL SR MICHEL ANGELO MARESI DA CARAVAGGIO IN MALTA 1608'. See London 2005, cat. no. 8, with extensive bibliography.

46. Baldinucci 1681–1728, ed. 1846, IV, p. 206. The passage concerns the façade of Palazzo dell'Antella, for which see below.

47. See Marini 2001, cat. no. 14, who illustrates the *Sleeping Cupid* in the Indianapolis Museum of Art as the probable subject of Murtola's poem. However, see below.

48. First published in Stone 1997[2], pp. 167–8: 'stimando io ora molto più di prima il mio cupido poi che mi viene lodato da Vostra Signoria alla quale bacio le mani … ' ABF, Filza 46, f. 756r. As mentioned in my article, the letter mostly concerns the application of the Buonarroti brothers' nephew, Lionardo Barducci (1600–1625), to be admitted to Wignacourt's *paggeria*. For further documents on this initiative, see now also Cole 2005, esp. pp. 18–19, who notes in passing that in December 1623 Michelangelo il giovane used his influence with the Barberini to try to get Fra Francesco Buonarroti confirmed as secretary of the Order of St John (BAV, Fondo Barb. Lat., 6460, f. 23).

49. Michelangelo's *Cupid* statue was in Mantua in the early Seicento; perhaps Caravaggio knew copies after it. See Puglisi 1998, p. 296. See also Rubenstein 1986.

50. For further interpretations, in addition to Stone 1997[2], see Posèq 1987; Cropper 1991, pp. 199–201; and especially Puglisi 1998, pp. 294–7.

51. On Caravaggio's satirical character, see Stone 2002.

52. Puglisi 1998, 296–7.

53. Marini 2001, p. 544.

54. Stone 1997[2]. On the Antellesi, cf. also Cole 2005.

55. The painter of the Clowes copy after the *Sleeping Cupid* (see below) seems to interpret the lower area as a stone ledge or slab. The Pitti canvas has darkened, and it would be hazardous to claim exactly what the putto is sleeping on.

56. Stone 1997[2], n. 19.

57. I thank Donald J. LaRocca for this information. Dell'Antella, like Wignacourt, was no doubt a connoisseur of arms and armour. The Commendatore's beautiful gilded *coltellaccio* (long hunting knife) is preserved in the Museo Bardini in Florence. See Cardini 2004, cat. no. 73.

58. The appearance of an unstrung Turkish bow – even in the context of a sleeping Cupid – could be interpreted in Malta as a conceit for the demise of the Order's arch-enemy, the Turks. But Caravaggio may have chosen it simply to provide the picture with an exotic element.

59. I am much obliged to K. Christiansen for this observation.

60. Macioce 1994.

61. Though Baldinucci calls it a 'cigno' or swan. See Pizzorusso 1983; and Sebregondi 2005, p. XLIX.

62. Christiansen–Mann 2001, cat. no. 70.

63. 75 x 140 cm. Attributed to Caracciolo by W. Prohaska. The picture was recently restored, removing a loincloth that had been added at a later date.

64. 76.8 cm x 102.2 cm. Sebregondi 2005, p. L, fig. 5, and nn. 83–85. Published in colour in Mojana 1996, pp. 36–7.

65. 65.5 x 105.5 cm. Inv. IMA–CL 10016.

66. Marini 2001, cat. no. 14, illus. in colour. See also Marini, in *Il Cinquecento Lombardo* 2000, pp. 480–1.

67. Sebregondi 2005, p. L, and n. 86, mentions another, and much smaller version of the *Sleeping Cupid* in a private collection in Rome (61.5 x 52 cm).

68. 118.5 x 95.5 cm. The early provenance of this work is unknown. See Chiarini–Padovani 2003, vol. 2, cat. no. 156, for the later history of the picture's whereabouts. An engraving after the work is illustrated in London 2005, cat. no. 9, p. 120. Marini 2001, cat. no. 95, p. 318, illustrates a painted copy of the canvas (after 1650?).

69. Gash 1997, p. 159.

70. Marini 2001, p. 318, seems to think it is 'parzialmente non finito', an idea I do not share. I think the picture is finished, in a style that anticipates the great Sicilian works.

71. For a full technical report, see Gregori 1991, pp. 318–24; and Gregori 1997, pp. 124–31.

72. Gregori 1974.

73. Fabbri 2005, esp. pp. LXVI–LXVII, unconvincingly argues that the Pitti portrait represents Wignacourt. The man in the Pitti portrait is much older than Wignacourt, and his physiognomy is entirely different. Wignacourt's head is rounder, his ears slightly smaller, his skin colour lighter, his cheeks more full and healthy, his beard thicker and darker. The knight in the Pitti canvas looks like a typical Florentine

with high cheekbones and a fine aristocratic nose (Wignacourt's nose is not as handsome). A crime lab should be able to settle this issue once and for all using the latest imaging technology. The resemblance between the two men is nothing more than the Morellian consistency with which Caravaggio, at this moment, constructs heads of older types.

74. Bologna 1992, p. 478, n. 23; cf. also Gregori 1991, p. 318.
75. Chiarini 1989 (as in the villa at Poggio Imperiale). Sebregondi 2005, n. 133, remarks that the 1696 inventory was actually of the contents of the villa at Artimino.
76. Gash 1997; and Sciberras 2002². See also London 2005, cat. no. 9; Sebregondi 2005; and Fabbri 2005.
77. Sciberras 2002², pp. 11–12. Sebregondi 2005, p. LII, states on the basis of a new document (ABF, Filza 114, f. 256r), that he departed the convent on 25 October 1608.
78. Fabbri 2005, p. LXVI, and n. 19
79. Fabbri 2005, p. LXXI. Martelli was certainly there until early September 1609, when he apparently told Cosimo del Sera that he wanted to leave.
80. Sebregondi 2005, p. LIII. However, Litta gives the death date as 5 November 1618; see Fabbri 2005, p. LXVII, and n. 29.
81. Fabbri 2005, p. LXVI, and n. 19: 'Ieri comparsero qua le galere di Malta e con esse il Sig.r Priore Martelli, che sebbene è invecchiato assai, di salute sta però benissimo'.
82. Oil on canvas. 117 x 157 cm. This discussion is based on London 2005, cat. no. 7, with previous bibl.; and Sciberras–Stone 2005².
83. Briefly in the 1990s, it was placed back in its old position in the Chapel of Italy. See fig. 13 above for a photograph of this hanging.
84. Sciberras–Stone 2005², fig. 4.
85. Marangoni 1922, p. 41, and pl. XXXIX. Perhaps independently, Gabriel Rouchès (1920) came to the same conclusion, though, surprisingly, he thought the St Jerome was painted in Rome. See Berne–Joffroy 1999, p. 148.
86. Carità 1957.
87. For an exciting account of the theft by someone at the center of the recovery effort, see Zerafa 2004.
88. See ICR 1991 for a technical report. The picture was not lent to the Naples–London exhibitions in 2004–2005.
89. The copy contains the monogram G.NF.D.C. See Sciberras–Stone 2005², n. 6.
90. Hess 1958; Macioce 1987; and Sciberras–Stone 2005².
91. As mentioned above, the matter of identifying the page is complex.
92. Macioce 1987, p. 178; Sciberras–Stone 2005², n. 30.
93. Macioce 1994, pp. 217, 228; Sciberras–Stone 2005², p. 10.
94. Sciberras–Stone 2005², pp. 10–13.
95. A recently published document discovered by Sciberras shows that the Jerome and Magdalene were given new frames in 1661 and that the two other Malaspina pictures were removed at this time. It is likely that only in 1661 were the Jerome and Magdalene placed above the arches of the passageways. Thus, Bellori's informant probably saw the works after this date. See Sciberras–Stone 2005², pp. 10–13.
96. The picture, which is best seen from the entrance to the hall, where its figures seem literally to inhabit the space above the altar, measures 3.61 x 5.20 metres. It has been suggested that at some point, perhaps during Preti's renovations to the Oratory in the 1680s, Caravaggio's canvas was trimmed some 18–20 cm along the left edge; see Florence 1999, pp. 17-18, 28.
97. Though I think it is possible that the sword in the Borghese David bears Caravaggio's initials (a conceit imitated, I now realise, by Orazio Gentileschi in his Executioner with the Head of John the Baptist, Madrid, Prado, c. 1612–13). See Stone 2002, p. 33, and n. 66. I do not believe, incidentally, that the 'f.' in the Beheading signature, which precedes the name rather than follows it, stands for 'fecit'. Given the Maltese context, this surely means 'fra'.
98. See Florence 1999 for a technical report.
99. Cutajar 1989.
100. It must have been completed before 27 August, the date Caravaggio was named as an accomplice in the tumulto. See the previous chapter for a detailed account.

101. See Stone 1997[1]; and Sciberras 1999. I would, however, like to make one correction. I later found that there was, in fact, a large passageway connecting the church to the Oratory, as AOM, Arch. 105 (Lib. Conc. 1613–16), f. 42v, makes clear: [4 March 1614 new style; 1613 ab incarnat.], 'Die eadem. Monsignor Illustrissimo et il Venerando Consiglio hanno concesso che il molto Reverendo Signor Prior della Chiesa fra Pietro Urrea Camarasa possi erigere un'Altare ad honor di San Carlo Borromeo nella Capella della Chiesa posta avanti l'intrata grande dell'Oratorio di San Giovanni Decollato'.

102. See Stone 1997[1], who also discusses the lunette painting shown in the Kilian print. The actual lunette still exists in Rabat, where it was identified by Mons. J. Azzopardi. The painting, which I attribute to Bartolomeo Garagona, was probably inserted above the *Beheading* in c. 1620–30.

103. For the suggestion that the architectural setting is inspired by a print from the knights' statute book illustrating the punishment for capital crimes, see Stone 1997[1].

104. '… e per la Chiesa di San Giovanni gli fece dipingere la Decollazione del Santo caduto a terra, mentre il carnefice, quasi non l'abbia colpito alla prima con la spada, prende il coltello dal fianco, afferrandolo ne' capelli per distaccargli la testa dal busto. Riguarda intenta Erodiade, ed una vecchia seco inorridisce allo spettacolo, mentre il guardiano della prigione in abito turco addita l'atroce scempio. In quest'opera il Caravaggio usò ogni potere del suo pennello, avendovi lavorato con tanta fierezza che lasciò in mezze tinte l'imprimitura della tela . . .' (Bellori, in Hibbard 1983, pp. 368–9).

105. He also remarked, quite accurately, on how thinly painted the work is (see the previous note). By the 1660s, when it is likely Bellori wrote this section of the biography, there may have been painted copies of the *Beheading* in Italy he could have seen. But only a confrontation with the actual canvas or a description by a careful observer would have yielded such detailed information about Caravaggio's technique. Could there have been more than one informant who helped Bellori?

106. For a broad iconographic investigation of Caravaggio's treatment of the Baptist in his art, see Treffers 2000.

107. Calvesi 1990, p. 367.

108. The greenish-blue jacket called an 'abito turco' by Bellori is not an Ottoman costume. The very idea that anything Turkish would be represented in an altarpiece depicting the tragic death of the patron saint of the Order – in their conventual church no less – is too fantastic to entertain. It is much more likely, I think, that Bellori's informant meant to imply that the costume was painted in turquoise colour, that is, 'turchino'. A true 'abito turco' would include a turban as part of an entirely different costume.

109. Because Salome is not named in the Bible, writers frequently referred to her, erroneously, by her mother's name, Herodias. The recent restoration of the picture has made it much easier to see that the girl has a large apron tied to her waist that swings forward as she stoops to receive the head. Thus, she is probably a servant in Herod's palace.

110. This prison window type was known in the Seicento as a '*misericordia*'. I thank John Beldon Scott for pointing this out to me.

111. 285 x 205 cm. See Marini 2001, cat. no. 101; Spike 2001, cat. no. 71; and London 2005, cat. no. 15 – all with prev. bibl. The 'Maltese' character of the *Annunciation* came into sharp focus for me when seeing the work in the context of the Naples exhibition. I thank K. Sciberras, who recently examined the picture in Nancy in preparation for an essay on the Lorraines in Malta, for sharing his observations with me. He also supports a Malta-period dating. We both thank Sophie Harent, curator at Nancy, for her assistance.

112. It seems unlikely that Caravaggio began the *Annunciation* in Malta and then completed it in Sicily, since we have no reason to suspect that his personal items were shipped to him, let alone taken by him personally as he escaped from Fort St Angelo. If he painted the work during one or more of his brief stays in Syracuse, Messina, Palermo and Naples, he would have had difficulty corresponding with his patrons and arranging for the picture to be shipped to Lorraine. Malta, therefore, remains the most likely place for the commission and its execution.

113. I am grateful to K. Christiansen and D. Carr for their comments on the picture's state

of preservation. According to a 1970 report, in 1968–9, ICR in Rome relined the canvas and removed extensive 19th-century overpaint except in two areas, the upper part of the angel's wings and the central part of the basket. Probably repainted before 1800, these areas have no original pigment underlying them. Inpainting by ICR was done in watercolour; some of the Virgin's face is reconstructed in *tratteggio*.

114. I was fortunate to discuss this problem with J. Gash at the Caravaggio Study Day in March 2005 at the National Gallery, London. The Jailor's *abito* has some purple in it, which the Madonna's drapery does not.

115. '… si che, oltre l'onore della croce, il Gran Maestro gli pose al collo una ricca collana d'oro e gli fece dono di due schiavi, con altre dimostrazioni della stima e compiacimento dell'operar suo' (Bellori, in Hibbard 1983, p. 369).

116. Probably engraved by Albert Clouwet, a French printmaker active in Rome in 1644–67 in the workshop of C. Bloemaert. See Bellori 1672 (ed. 1976), p. 89, n. 2.

Fig. 34. *Supper at Emmaus*, Milan, Pinacoteca di Brera

CHAPTER FOUR

Malta in Late Caravaggio:
A Chronology for the Final Years

Keith Sciberras

The exciting context of Caravaggio's life from his turbulent escape from Rome to his untimely death, witnessed what were perhaps the most significant pictorial activities that were taking place outside Rome between 1606 and 1610. This short span of time, during which Caravaggio moved respectively through Naples, Malta, Sicily and once again Naples, has been romantically referred to as Caravaggio's 'final years'.[1]

Within those four years, and for a very brief moment in the magnificent history of Italian art, Malta was set to play a prominent role. It was a period when Caravaggio, a fugitive yearning to return to Rome, produced outstanding masterpieces. Within this charged and dramatic setting, his stay in Malta, as discussed in detail in the preceding chapters,[2] provided the artist with his only long and real moment of tranquility, a period when the artist reflected on both his life and his work. The Maltese paintings of *St Jerome* (pl. IV) and the *Beheading of St John the Baptist* (pl. VIII) bear brilliant testimony to this.

Caravaggio had arrived in Malta less than fourteen months after murdering Ranuccio Tomassoni, and, away from the crowded commotion of a sprawling Naples, the compact city of Valletta, so small in comparison, became a haven for the artist. Away from his artistic rivals, reflecting on his art, and ambitiously painting his largest picture so far, he also sought political alliances that would help him achieve his ultimate objective of setting foot once more in Rome. However, after the sudden drama of the brawl in August 1608, subsequent detention in September, and his break-out in early October, Caravaggio's 'restful' period was over. His creativity and art were necessarily dogged by the turbulent circumstances that followed.

The great pictures that Caravaggio produced in his final years are the culmination of a powerful style that had taken Rome by storm. By 1606, his style had evolved considerably, obviously conditioned by the very character of his own life. Despite the rough and tumble of his daily life and the image of a macho artist that was inevitably created around him, the artist produced inventions of extraordinary religious intensity; in many instances he rethought the traditional iconographical approach to his religious subjects. His was a search for profound drama highlighted by pockets of light and shade that hit the canvas with inventions of striking intensity.

This final chapter is an attempt at establishing a chronology for the pictures that the artist painted in these eventful last four years of his life. Chronology, for an artist who painted with vigour and nerve, is difficult to securely pin down and it is obviously subject to pitfalls, arguments, and disagreement.[3] It is, as all know, dangerous ground and subject to change. Caravaggio's art changed so rapidly; he rethought his methods and technical approach. His brushwork achieved greater liberty of execution and in his post-1608 works he frequently utilised the reddish-brown preparation as middleground, and thus as part of the final pictorial surface. At times he worked in different styles whilst in the same place; the mood of the subject was reflected in his working method. The two great altar paintings that he executed in Messina, and discussed briefly below, are a case in point. In the early eighteenth century, this diversity attracted the attention of the Sicilian biographer Francesco Susinno in his discussion of the artist's Sicilian paintings.[4]

On at least two occasions during this unsettled period, that is in the hasty flight from Rome and in the dramatic escape from Malta, it is highly probable that Caravaggio left his preferred brushes, pigment pots, canvas rolls, and palette behind. In Rome, moreover, he left behind his friends and the models that he had been painting from life. In these circumstances, any artist must experience a sense of loss, even of direction and a negative psychological feeling of having to 'start afresh'.

In his post-Roman years Caravaggio's models are different; many are not real personages taken directly from nature but are images that inhabit his mind. Thus they appear in paintings that he painted in different locations. The jailer in the Malta *Beheading*, for example, is more or less the man holding a handkerchief in the *Burial of St Lucy*

(Museo di Palazzo Bellomo, Syracuse) painted just some weeks later in Sicily (fig. 17). The head of the Malta *St Jerome* has striking similarities to that of the earlier St Andrew in the Neapolitan *Crucifixion of St Andrew* (The Cleveland Museum of Art, Cleveland), whilst the female image that he uses for Salome (or her maid) in the *Beheading*, for the Virgin in the Nancy *Annunciation of the Virgin* (pl. XXII), for Magdalene in the *Raising of Lazarus* (fig. 36), and for the Virgin in the *Adoration of the Shepherds* (fig. 7; Museo Regionale, Messina) belongs to one typology. These, however, obviously do not mean that Caravaggio abandoned the method of painting directly from reality. In the depiction of certain emphatic poses and gestures the artist seems to have painted directly from life.

Stylistic, technical, documentary, and contextual research carried out on the corpus of Caravaggio's late works provides, despite controversies, enough ground for a more than tentative chronology. We cannot be firmer than that. There are pictures which fit in perfectly within a stylistic continuum. Others seem to defy time and location and cannot (without the availability of precise documents) be securely pinned down to a precise date.

The circumstances and activity of Caravaggio during his first weeks in exile after Rome in mid-1606, protected in the Lazio regions of Paliano, Palestrina, or even Zagarolo, are still difficult to assemble. Of the pictures that he painted during this time, only the *Supper at Emmaus* (Pinacoteca di Brera, Milan)[5] can be held as a probable reference point (fig. 34), even though its power can also fit a slightly later date. Compared with his earlier treatment of the same subject in the *Supper at Emmaus* (National Gallery, London), its profound and introverted intensity marks it as a veritable icon of this new phase. There are no early documents for this work, but it is most likely the picture that Caravaggio's early biographers Mancini and Bellori mention as having been painted in this period.

On the other hand, a painting of the *Magdalene*, although well known through copies and mentioned by Baglione, Mancini, and Bellori as similarly painted in this time, remains elusive. It surely cannot be identified with a painting (Private Collection, Rome) presented as autograph in recent years; this picture is instead a contemporary copy.[6] Caravaggio's *Magdalene* immediately achieved great popularity and was widely copied; it is a haunting image, an evocation of the artist's personal drama, an intimate reflection of his own distress. The artist probably took the painting to Naples. It is also probable that it was deposited there until he took it back with him on his last and ill-fated sea voyage in July 1610; a *Magdalene* is documented as being amongst Caravaggio's belongings on board the felucca on which he was travelling.

Caravaggio's painting of *St Francis in Meditation* (Museo Civico, Cremona), proposed as dating to this period,[7] is a thorny one, not in its autograph status, but in its precise dating. It is an undocumented picture; its provenance can only be traced back to the first half of the nineteenth century. In the treatment of the background there is a direct link with the Roman years, but the face of Francis and his pose is that of the new developments announced in the Brera *Supper at Emmaus*. The saint's crouching position, one elbow rested on the knee, hands grasped together and the head resting on them, was in Caravaggio's mind when he pondered about and then painted the cripple cast in shadow at bottom left in the *Seven Works of Mercy* (Pio Monte della Misericordia, Naples) of late 1606 (fig. 6). The *St Francis* beautifully encompasses the character of the artist's early post-Roman work, even though its dating remains the subject of controversy.

The chronology of Caravaggio's large religious paintings emerges with considerable clarity, even though the mechanics of patronage of three of them, namely the *Virgin of the Rosary* (Kunsthistorisches Museum, Vienna), the Cleveland *Crucifixion of St Andrew*, and the Nancy *Annunciation of the Virgin*, are still not precisely established. The greatest problem is certainly that posed by the *Virgin of the Rosary*, a picture traditionally held to be an early Neapolitan work, but stylistically and technically much closer to his Roman period. The latter view, in which the picture is being seen as belonging to the Roman phase, has recently gained considerable ground in Caravaggio scholarship;[8] the fact that the *Virgin of the Rosary* was on sale in Naples in September 1607 does not necessarily mean that it was actually painted there. In any case, this is a classic example where a picture's early provenance can, at times, complicate matters. Its patron, immortalized by Caravaggio in the lower left corner, similarly remains difficult to identify.

Caravaggio had moved south to Naples in the last days of the summer of 1606. There he immediately embraced a new network of patrons and prolifically embarked in the production of large scale works. The first documented of these works is generally

Fig. 35. *Flagellation*, Naples, Museo di Capodimonte

considered lost. On 6 October, Caravaggio received a hefty advance payment for an altarpainting of the *Virgin and Child with Sts Dominic, Francis, Nicholas, and Vito* to measure more than 3.5 metres high.[9] Commissioned by Niccolò Radolovich, this picture is still surrounded by mystery and has not yet been successfully identified, even if it has also been (wrongly, in my opinion) associated with the *Virgin of the Rosary*. It is not known, however, whether Caravaggio had actually ever handed in the work. The point being pressed here is on whether it should be considered a 'lost' picture. Knowing how, between 1606–1607, the artist had conned the Duke of Modena's Ambassador in Rome into delaying and never consigning a picture on which he had taken a deposit,[10] it is also possible that Caravaggio left Naples without actually delivering the Radolovich picture. Throughout the artist's first Neapolitan period, and by May 1607, Cesare d'Este Duke of Modena, was furious about how his Ambassador had been treated by Caravaggio, how he had been 'fooled' into interminable prolongations over the delivery of his picture. The Radolovich picture could have been a similar case.

Two well documented altarpaintings from Caravaggio's first Neapolitan phase are the beautifully controlled *Flagellation of Christ* (fig. 35; Museo di Capodimonte, Naples) and the impressively realistic re-interpretation of the theme of the *Seven Works of Mercy*. These altarpaintings show how Caravaggio had managed to overcome the shock of the Tomassoni murder, and how he could approach large canvases with such concentration, intensity of vision and spiritual understanding. Caravaggio received payment for the *Seven Works of Mercy* in January 1607, whilst payments for the *Flagellation*, executed for Tommaso de Franchis, date to May 1607 (documented payments do not specifically identify the picture).[11] The invention for the *Flagellation* was tremendously successful and it was probably just after this that he painted a smaller horizontal version of the subject (Musée des Beaux-Arts, Rouen) for an unknown patron. Both paintings are perfect companions to another altarpainting, the undocumented *Crucifixion of St Andrew* in Cleveland.[12]

The *St Andrew* thus probably dates to late 1606 or early 1607; suggestions that this painting could date to the late Neapolitan period (1609–1610) are not endorsed here. The contextual problem with this work is that its early provenance, though clearly associated with the Conde de Benavente, Viceroy of Naples between 1603 and 1610, does not, on its own, serve to securely tie it down to any one of Caravaggio's two Neapolitan periods. Dating must thus be based on stylistic and technical grounds. Proponents for a late date consider mainly the expressive treatment of the saint's body which, it is true, is different in handling to that of the Christ in the *Flagellation*. This, however, happens in other occasions, where Caravaggio approaches the handling of pigment in a different manner even though painting pictures within a relatively close period. In both works, the tormentors, on the other hand, show remarkably similar handling and solid brushwork.

The next phase in this chronology is the Maltese period, July 1607 – October 1608. Given the amount of time Caravaggio spent on the island, the corpus of pictures dating from Malta, discussed in detail in the previous chapter, is undeniably small. The *Beheading of St John the Baptist*, the *St Jerome*, and the *Portrait of Alof de Wignacourt and a Page* (pl. I), are milestone pictures which perfectly sum up his Maltese temperament. The vastness of the *Beheading*, spread out on an enormous canvas, was a challenge that Caravaggio probably set out himself. It was a scale that was more appropriate to mural painting, a scale that he had never ever previously attempted. He worked fast and expressively exploited the preparation of the canvas as middleground (fig. 41). In many ways, the *Beheading* ambitiously, and successfully, extended the east-end space of the Oratory of San Giovanni Decollato for where it was painted. In this painting, the street like appearance that he had earlier envisaged for the *Seven Works of Mercy*, with figures roaming by as if in a busy Neapolitan alley, made way for an arrangement of figures dictated by a calculated geometric composition. The vastness of space itself, in turn, paved the way for the later Sicilian altarpieces of the *Burial of St Lucy* and the *Raising of Lazarus*.

Any doubts regarding the autograph status of the Pitti *Portrait of a Knight* (pl. XX), probably the last known portrait that Caravaggio painted (excluding self-portraits painted within religious compositions), have by now been fully settled. Undocumented, the picture was only identified and attributed to the artist in the mid-1960s. It has since then featured with controversy in both attribution and identification of the sitter. The association of the sitter with Grand Master Wignacourt should be abandoned,[13] in favour of the plausible suggestion that the man is Fra Antonio Martelli.

The Pitti canvas was most likely painted in the winter months of late 1607, or probably early 1608; perhaps it is a coincidence, but it is in this period that Martelli (if it is him) started thinking of leaving the island. The *Portrait of a Knight* and the *Portrait of Wignacourt* are the only two portraits that can be securely identified as belonging to Caravaggio's late years, even though there are notable technical differences in how Caravaggio executed both paintings. The portrait

Fig. 36. *Raising of Lazarus*, Messina, Museo Regionale

of Wignacourt was an 'official' state portrait and is highly finished in treatment. The portrait of a Knight, on the other hand, is a more intimate 'household' portrait, almost fugitive in nature. Close in date, but painted with more pigment, is the Pitti *Sleeping Cupid* (pl. XVII). In turn, this is the only known mythological picture belonging to his late years. An inscription on the reverse dating the work to 1608 is no doubt accurate.

Similarly, 1608 is most likely to be the date for the undocumented Nancy *Annunciation of the Virgin*. A Maltese provenance for this

114

remarkable but unfortunately ruined painting is forcefully argued for above in the preceding chapters. Painted for the Lorraines, the painting was probably commissioned by the Duke's son, Charles of Lorraine, Conte de Brie and Knight of Malta, who was on the island in 1608. In its rapid handling of brushwork, it is fascinatingly similar to the *Beheading*. It should thus date to the same period and, it may be observed, it bears the same hallmark of an exercise in mathematical construction.

After Malta, disgraced and still a fugitive but not at all secretive about his whereabouts, the restless Caravaggio was in Sicily moving between Syracuse, Messina, and Palermo.[14] Strangely, he does not travel immediately north to mainland Italy, to the Naples that had given him fortune but embeds himself in Sicily for some twelve months. The Sicilian period was to be a particularly productive period.

The three great works of this period, namely the *Burial of St Lucy*, painted late in 1608, the Messina *Raising of Lazarus* (fig. 36), and the *Adoration of the Shepherds* (fig. 7), painted in 1609, echo the power of Caravaggio's art in their brilliant concept of compositional space. It is indeed incredible how the artist could move from the constrained masterpiece of the *Beheading* to the astounding dramatization of the *Lazarus*, or how, within the space of a couple of weeks he could paint the *Adoration* so different in character to the *Lazarus*. The sadly ruined state of the *St Lucy* and the *Lazarus* unfolds more drama; unfortunately, their state of preservation does not help much in comparative work with the smaller paintings.

The *St Lucy* was painted when Caravaggio was once again on the run, a fugitive Knight of Malta, understandably looking over his shoulder with some apprehension. In such a situation it is simply incredible how the artist summoned the spirit to paint a picture measuring some four by three metres. Its sheer size is indeed an obvious indication that he was by no means in hiding. It was a bold statement, and Sicily was now to succumb to his art. The altarpaintings of the *Burial of St Lucy*, the *Raising of Lazarus* and the *Adoration of the Shepherds* together with the *Nativity with St Lawrence* (formerly Oratorio di San Lorenzo, Palermo; stolen in 1969 and not yet recovered), are the only surviving paintings that can be clearly documented to his Sicilian period. The artist is, however, known to have produced a number of easel paintings, even if their identification remains, in some instances, controversial.

At this stage Caravaggio's psychological state attracted the attention of Nicolo di Giacomo, who sometime before August 1609

Fig. 37. *Salome with the Head of St John the Baptist*, Madrid, Palacio Reale, Patrimonio Nacional

commissioned from him four paintings of the Passion of Christ. One of these, an unfortunately untraced painting representing *Christ carrying the Cross with the Virgin and two tormentors*, was actually delivered by the artist.[15] It could be that the other three pictures were never delivered. Dramatically, in his own note on the commission, di Giacomo describes Caravaggio as having a *cervello stravolto* (confused mind). Tension and strain were perhaps starting to take their toll, but this is also when Caravaggio charged his work with an even greater intensity. Soon after, the artist was on his way to Naples.

Why the artist had not felt the urge to return immediately to Naples in October 1608 remains somewhat of a mystery, a veil of which may perhaps be lifted by the fact that, on his return there a year later, in October 1609, he was badly manhandled and beaten. The cause of this brutal attack, which left him scarred, remains, however, unknown. The second Neapolitan phase started off on a bad note and ended even more tragically.

A fascinating group of outstanding easel pictures, generally held to be very late works, provide more dating problems than certainties: the two versions of *Salome with the Head of St John the Baptist* (Palacio

116

Fig. 38. *Salome receiving the Head of St John the Baptist,* London, The National Gallery

Reale, Madrid; The National Gallery, London), *David with the Head of Goliath* (Galleria Borghese, Rome), *St John the Baptist* (Galleria Borghese, Rome), the *Denial of Peter* (The Metropolitan Museum of Art, New York), and the *Martyrdom of St Ursula* (Banca Intesa, Naples). Only one of these is securely dated to the second Neapolitan period; the others fluctuate between 1606/07 and 1610.

The important fixed reference for dating these works is that set by the powerful and haunting *Martyrdom of St Ursula* (fig. 40), unfortunately ruined but emerging with new surprises following the removal of overpainting during a recent restoration. This picture was painted in Naples during the artist's last weeks of life and is well documented to May 1610.[16] In both style and rapid technique, it draws very close to it the undocumented *Denial of St Peter*. The latter, a masterpiece in the articulation of gestures, should thus be a very late work and of Neapolitan origin. It is painted thinly over the preparation, just like the *St Ursula*, with strong dabs of paint in the white highlights. It is with these dramatic highlights, in which the brush struck the canvas with

117

Fig. 39. *David with the Head of Goliath*, Rome, Galleria Borghese

vigour, that Caravaggio very selectively modeled the figures and dramatised the representation.

In the Borghese *St John the Baptist*, the boy is a loner who looks out at the spectators with a perturbing intensity; this picture has a technical solidity and a character that is perplexingly different to that of the *St Ursula*. If it was one of the two *St John* pictures that Caravaggio is known to have had with him on the felucca during his last unfortunate trip (as documents of 1611 suggest), then it was probably not painted in his last weeks of life. Some scholars have said that the *St John* was made for Cardinal Borghese to appease him and hope for Papal pardon. Even if this was the case, it does not necessarily mean that the picture dates to 1610.

Similarly, the Borghese *David* (fig. 39) is haunting and problematic. It is one of those pictures which, like others painted by the artist, simply cannot easily be placed in a secure date. Traditionally, and rather romantically, it is held to be Caravaggio's last picture and its drama fits in perfectly with this, but such dating may need to be reviewed.[17] Its power spans the entire four years of his late period; its uncertain early history makes it even more enigmatic.

Of the two interpretations of *Salome with the Head of the Baptist*, the one in Madrid (fig. 37), so forceful in its composition and solid treatment of mass and space, is probably the earlier and possibly dates as early as the first Neapolitan period (in Naples, it was greatly admired by Battistello Caracciolo, who was inspired by it for his own work). Again, the early history of these works is not known and both are the subject of considerable debate.[18] The London *Salome* (fig. 38) is probably post-Malta, and in its handling of paint and utilisation of the preparation it is undeniably close to the Sicilian works. In this, it could possibly be identified as the picture that Bellori claims Caravaggio painted in order to placate Grand Master Wignacourt after his escape (even though Bellori mentions Herodiade with the head of John in a basin, rather than Salome: *Cercando insieme di placare il Gran Maestro, gli mandò in dono un mezza figura di herodiade con la testa di San Giovanni nel bacino*). The painting mentioned by Bellori, however, does not seem to have ever made it to Malta.

Caravaggio's second Neapolitan sojourn is a period of easel paintings; badly injured following the tavern brawl, he hardly had the energy to paint and remained in convalescence at the palace of his long-time protector the Marchesa Costanza Sforza Colonna. Regaining his health, he is securely documented to have painted only one picture, the *Martyrdom of St Ursula*. He surely must have painted others. He departed from Naples in July 1610, almost sure that a Papal pardon was finally being conceded. He would, however, never make it to Rome.[19] This was to be his last voyage. With him, amongst other things, he had at least three pictures, two representing *St John* and a *Magdalene*. Following a brief detention in prison at Palo and a hurried

Fig. 40. *Martyrdom of St Ursula*, Naples, Palazzo Zevallos, Banca Intesa collection

move north, the now tragic Caravaggio died most probably of fever at the age of 39, miserably deserted at Port' Ercole.

In quantifying the number of extant paintings dating to Caravaggio's final years, there is universal agreement on a corpus of the twenty-one fully autograph pictures discussed above, or twenty-two if the stolen *Nativity with St Lawrence* is included in the group.[20] This includes nine altarpaintings and thirteen easel pictures, of which two are portraits. Whilst this corpus is held as closed by many scholars, there are others who open Caravaggio's oeuvre to include a small number of other pictures and inventions. Three paintings, namely the *David with the Head of Goliath* (Kunsthistorisches Museum, Vienna), the *St John the Baptist* (Private Collection, Munich), and the *Toothpuller* (Pitti Palace, Florence) fit within this controversial context.[21] Whilst the *David* could indeed be an original of c. 1606/1607 (even though problematically painted on panel), the *St John the Baptist* has been little seen and has yet to be properly exhibited. The *Toothpuller* remains a controversial picture. While it has strong points of contact with Caravaggio's very late work there are also notable differences.[22]

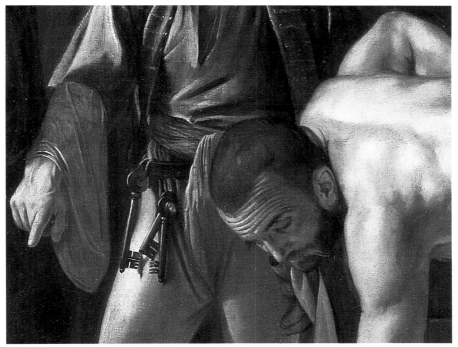

Fig. 41. *The Beheading of St John the Baptist*, Valletta, Oratory of San Giovanni Decollato, detail

   In the recent years a number of other paintings have been presented as 'new proposals'. None of them, in my opinion, is really worth the qualifier as a Caravaggio original. Two versions of the *St John at the Spring*, an *Ecce Homo*, and a *Salome*, all from private collections, are amongst these *nuove proposte*.[23] Even though the *Ecce Homo* is not by the artist, its invention seems correct and Caravaggio might have painted an original of this very same composition – probably in Sicily – that has yet to be discovered. The invention for the *St John at the Spring* is more problematic and it is debatable whether Caravaggio ever painted an original. Another version of this *St John at the Spring* is in Malta; this picture has been, in the past, attributed to Caravaggio but the attribution no longer has any validity. On the other hand, the invention for the *Salome* is almost certainly not Caravaggio's. Apart from these, there are other pictures that have been controversially attributed to Caravaggio. For the purpose of this study, note should be made on the painting of a *St Jerome* (Worcester Art Museum), held to be bought from Malta in the mid-twentieth century.[24] Its attribution to Caravaggio has been supported by some scholars,[25] but this very

121

interesting picture is definitely not by the artist. It is the work of a very close follower who probably had first hand knowledge of Caravaggio's Maltese and Sicilian works. The picture deserves greater study once it is restored.

Caravaggio's reputation as a portrait painter was always great but, unfortunately, few are the portraits that can be securely attributed to him. This is indeed an area where more research needs to be undertaken and where, surely, the corpus of portraits attributed to the artist has to be enlarged. A number of these portraits are well documented and are at present considered 'lost'. These include an oval portrait of Grand Master Wignacourt mentioned in the preceding chapter. Proposals for new portraits are currently met with misgivings; some still need to be properly exhibited. One such work is the *Portrait of a Man* (Private Collection). Stylistically, this painting is closer to Caravaggio's Roman (more than the first Neapolitan) period but it still needs to be exhibited and studied in greater detail.[26]

Moreover, there is still debate on other proposed inventions by the artist known only through hypothetical copies. The *Judith with the Head of Holofernes* (Museo Pignatelli, Naples) is a case in point. Even though it is well documented that a picture of this subject by Caravaggio was on sale in Naples in 1607,[27] it is debatable whether this painting, attributed by some to Louis Finson, is a perfect replica of Caravaggio's lost work. Later seventeenth and eighteenth century inventories, other documents and sources refer to other pictures that Caravaggio possibly painted in his last years. Whilst some references are no doubt incorrect, the probability that other paintings by the artist are just waiting to be 'rediscovered' is indeed considerable.

Recent exhibitions on Caravaggio's 'final years' provided a perfect context for assessing the role played by Caravaggio's Malta. They have provided a visual experience that is certainly unrepeatable in the years to come. This coincided with great research interest in the Maltese period; research which has now moved into a phase of deeper and wider understanding. However, despite the growing knowledge on the subject and new documentary discoveries there are still a number of questions that remain unanswered. In general, much is known and the number of personages with whom Caravaggio had contact has been considerably enlarged, but much also remains on the basis of hypothesis. The precise reasons why the artist came to

Malta, the personage who first addressed him towards the island, the Knights' support for full Papal pardon and eventual return to Rome, the reason for the eventful brawl, the circumstances for his escape, the extent of the Knights' vengeance, and the full corpus of pictures are still subjects of considerable debate. The speed of research is however fast and it is hoped that this book, *Caravaggio: Art, Knighthood, and Malta*, succeeds in bringing readers up to date with the latest scholarship.

NOTES

1. This period was recently the theme for an outstanding exhibition – *Caravaggio: The Final Years*. Those readers who had the privilege of visiting this marvelous exhibition in Naples (Museo di Capodimonte, Oct. 2004 – Feb. 2005) and London (National Gallery, Feb. 2005 – May 2005) and compared Caravaggio's paintings from the first Neapolitan period (late l606 – mid-1607) with those that he painted in Sicily (late 1608 – late 1609) and thereafter, would have realised how fundamentally important his stay in Malta was. The exhibition's ability to group together the great altarpieces of his pre and post-Malta years showed how crucial the *Beheading of St John the Baptist* (Oratory of San Giovanni Decollato, Valletta) was in his artistic development. Unfortunately, however, for a variety of reasons beyond the curators' role, this masterpiece from the Maltese period, together with two others, namely the *St Jerome Writing* (St John's Museum, Valletta), and the *Portrait of Alof de Wignacourt and a Page* (Louvre, Paris), were not exhibited in the show. This was the only major lacuna in a dazzling undertaking that will shape Caravaggio studies for the years to come. Only one other pivotal picture, the *Flagellation* (Musée des Beaux-Arts, Rouen), which dates to the first Neapolitan period, was missing.
2. The 'Maltese' pictures are here discussed only within the context of a chronology for Caravaggio's late years. For references, detailed bibliography, and further reading refer to those provided in Chapters 2 and 3 above.
3. The exhibition *Caravaggio: The Final Years* succeeded brilliantly in two major aspects. It differentiated between the autograph pictures and the unlikely (or in some instances 'impossible') attributions, and provided an invaluable side-by-side visual reference for attempting the formulation of a chronology for the period 1606–1610. This chronology is subject to considerable controversy and there is no universal agreement amongst Caravaggio scholars on the precise dating of a number of his 'undocumented' works.
4. For a transcription of Susinno (1724), see Macioce 2003, F.23, pp. 334-7.
5. For a bibliography and references on the pictures discussed in this essay see the respective catalogue entries in Naples 2004 and London 2005.
6. This controversial painting was not exhibited in *Caravaggio: The Final Years*. For this picture and an attribution to Caravaggio, see Pacelli 1994, pp. 161-97; Marini 2001, pp. 280-1, 507-9; and Marini 2003.
7. This proposed dating is strongly and convincingly argued for by Christiansen in Naples 2004, pp.104-6.
8. The painting was absent from the show. Prohaska, Christiansen, Benedetti and others are particularly firm in their assertion in favour of a Roman dating. Bologna in Naples 2004, discusses it within the Neapolitan context.
9. Pacelli 1994, pp. 16-19; for a transcription of the documents see Macioce 2003, II DOC 315, II DOC 317, II DOC 318.
10. For a transcription of the numerous references relating to this case, see Macioce 2003.
11. For a transcription of payments for the two pictures, see Macioce 2003, II DOC 326, II DOC 327, II DOC 338, II DOC 342.
12. These three pictures were shown side-by-side, for the first time, in the Naples exhibition, providing a brilliant opportunity for comparative study.

13. Despite being abandoned by the scholars who proposed this attribution, it has been recently put forward by Fabbri 2005, pp.LXVI-LXVII.

14. Dates for Caravaggio's movements between the Sicilian cities have not yet been completely settled, and his movements are more or less dated through circumstantial evidence and biographies.

15. For a transcription of the document see Macioce 2003, II DOC 319.

16. Pacelli 1994, pp. 100-17; for a transcription of the documents see also Macioce 2003, II DOC 399, II DOC 400.

17. Christiansen, Papi, and Stone believe the work dates to c. 1605–1606. Stone believes that the painting was done in the latest months of the Roman period or possibly in the immediate aftermath of the murder of Tomassoni during the summer of 1606. Longhi originally believed the *David* was a Roman period work; however by 1959 he changed his mind in favour of the second Naples period. See Christiansen 1990, p. 52; Papi in Gregori 1991, pp. 284-5; and Stone 2002 for a detailed review of these views.

18. It is here that in the exhibition in both Naples and London, the Maltese *St Jerome* was most sorely missed. Shown together these pictures would have provided visual data of great importance.

19. For a transcription of the documents relating to Caravaggio's final voyage and his death see Macioce 2003, II DOCs 404-409/a (excluding II DOC 408).

20. This count does not include the *Virgin of the Rosary* and the *Crowning with Thorns* (Kunsthistorisches Museum, Vienna). The latter is dated by Bologna, Pacelli and others to 1607.

21. These three pictures were not included in the exhibition. The *Holy Family with St John the Baptist* (Otero-Silva Collection, Caracas; in deposit at the Metropolitan Museum of Art, New York), dated by some scholars to c. 1607, probably dates to the Roman years. It is a remarkable, fully autograph picture.

22. Gregori and Christiansen, amongst others, believe the picture to be by Caravaggio.

23. These pictures were presented as such in the Naples exhibition. Also exhibited in Naples was the *St Francis* (Carpineto Romano, in deposit at Palazzo Barberini, Rome). The *St Francis* is a good work and technical analyses seem to point in an autograph direction, even if, rightly so, there continues to be much disagreement on its autograph status in favour of the somewhat stronger version in the Capuchin Church, Rome. In any case, however, this invention seems to belong to Caravaggio's late Roman years, rather than to the post-Roman phase. A good copy of this picture is in Malta (private collection), but this does not in any way suggest that Caravaggio's original could be associated with the island. The *nuove proposte* paintings did not make it to the London show, even though they are included in the English version of the catalogue.

24. Museum Files, Worcester Art Museum. I thank Dr James Welu and Ms Rita Albertson for their kind assistance in the study of this picture. The picture was bought in 1960 from New York, after being exported from Rome in 1958. Its earlier provenance is unclear, but an entry in the Museum file notes that it was found in Malta by Pico Cellini and Giuliano Briganti. Marini 2001, pp. 555-6, on the other hand, states that the picture belonged to the La Marca collection in Rome and had been transferred there from Naples. Prior to this, the picture, according to Marini, was in Messina.

25. Marini 2001, pp. 555-7. An attribution to Caravaggio had been pushed by Cellini, who restored it in the 1950s. At present, its attribution to Caravaggio is supported only by Marini. Museum correspondence shows that both Longhi and Mahon did not believe it to be by Caravaggio. Voss was inclined in favour of Caravaggio but he knew the picture only through a black and white photograph.

26. I know the picture only through a photograph. The attribution to Caravaggio has been well received by Gregori, Spike, and Christiansen. The picture was sold through Sotheby's New York, May 22, 1992, lot 193, as attributed to Battistello Caracciolo. See Gregori 1994, colour illustration p. 137; Spike 2001 (CD Rom), cat. no. 41.

27. The identification of this picture as a copy or replica after Caravaggio was first put forward by de Castris. This has been accepted by many scholars, even though there is still much debate on its authorship. See Bologna, in Naples 2004, p. 166.

BIBLIOGRAPHY

Age of Caravaggio 1985
  The Age of Caravaggio, ed. K. Christiansen, exh. cat.(New York: Metropolitan Museum of Art), New York, 1985.
Askew 1990
  Askew, P., *Caravaggio's Death of the Virgin*, Princeton, 1990.
Azzopardi 1978
  The Church of St. John in Valletta 1578–1978, ed. J. Azzopardi, exh. cat., Malta, 1978.
Azzopardi 1989[1]
  Azzopardi, J., "Documentary Sources on Caravaggio's Stay in Malta," in Farrugia Randon 1989, pp. 19-44.
Azzopardi 1989[2]
  Azzopardi, J., "Caravaggio's Admission into the Order: Papal Dispensation for the Crime of Murder," in Farrugia Randon 1989, pp. 45-56.
Azzopardi 1990
  St. Paul's Grotto: Church and Museum at Rabat, Malta, ed. J. Azzopardi, Malta, 1990.
Azzopardi 1996
  Azzopardi, J., "Un 'S. Francesco' di Caravaggio a Malta nel secolo XVIII: commenti sul periodo maltese del Merisi," in Macioce 1996, pp. 195-211.
Baldinucci 1681–1728
  Baldinucci, F., *Notizie dei professori del disegno . . .* , ed. F. Ranalli (ed. 1845–47), facsimile ed. by P. Barocchi, 7 vols, Florence, 1974-75.
Balsamo 1996
  Balsamo, J., "Les Caravage de Malte: le témoignage des voyageurs français (1616–1678)," in Gregori 1996, pp. 151-153.
Bandera 2000
  Bandera, M.C., "Caravaggio, Malta, e l'Ordine di San Giovanni," in Venice 2000, pp. 187-196.
Bell–Willette 2002
  Art History in the Age of Bellori: Scholarship and Cultural Politics in Seventeenth-Century Rome, eds. J. Bell and T. Willette, Cambridge, 2002.
Bellori 1672
  Bellori, G.P., *Le Vite de' pittori, scultori e architetti*, ed. E. Borea. Turin, 1976 (orig. Rome, 1672).
Bergamo 2000
  Caravaggio. La luce nella pittura lombarda, eds. C. Strinati and R. Vodret, exh. cat. (Bergamo), Milan, 2000.

Berne-Joffroy 1999
Berne-Joffroy, A., *Le Dossier Caravage: psychologie des attributions et psychologie de l'art*, 2nd ed., Paris, 1999.

Berra 2005
Berra, G., *Il Giovane Caravaggio in Lombardia: Ricerche documentarie sui Merisi, gli Aratori e i marchesi di Caravaggio*, Florence, 2005.

Bersani–Dutoit 1998
Bersani, L. and U. Dutoit, *Caravaggio's Secrets*, Cambridge (Mass.), 1998.

Bologna 1992
Bologna, F., *L'incredulità del Caravaggio*, Turin, 1992.

Bonello 2005
Bonello, G., "Caravaggio: Friends and Victims in Malta," in G. Bonello, *Histories of Malta: Ventures and Adventures*, vol. 6, Malta, 2005, pp. 67-79.

Borea 1970
Caravaggio e Caravaggeschi nelle gallerie di Firenze, ed. E. Borea, exh. cat. (Florence: Palazzo Pitti), Florence, 1970.

Bosio 1684
Bosio, G., *Dell'Istoria della Sacra Religione ...*, 3 vols., Rome (1594 [I-II] – 1602 [III]); ed. cit. 2nd ed. of vol. III, Naples (1684).

Bradford 1972
Bradford, E., *The Shield and the Sword: The Knights of St. John, Jerusalem, Rhodes and Malta*, London, 1972.

Buhagiar 1987
Buhagiar, M., *The Iconography of the Maltese Islands: 1400-1900, Painting*, Malta, 1987.

Calvesi 1987
L'Ultimo Caravaggio e la cultura artistica a Napoli in Sicilia e a Malta, ed. M. Calvesi, Syracuse, 1987.

Calvesi 1990
Calvesi, M., *Le Realtà del Caravaggio*, Turin, 1990.

Cardini 2004
Cardini, F., ed., *Monaci in armi: gli Ordini religioso-militari dai Templari alla Battaglia di Lepanto: Storia ed Arte*, exh. cat. (Rome: Castel Sant'Angelo), Rome, 2004.

Carità 1957
Carità, R., "Il restauro dei dipinti caravaggeschi della cattedrale di Malta," *Bollettino dell'Istituto Centrale del Restauro*, fasc. 29-30 (1957), pp. 41-82.

Carofano 2005
Luce e Ombra: caravaggismo e naturalismo nella pittura toscana del Seicento, ed. P. Carofano, exh. cat. (Pontedera), Florence, 2005.

Chiarini 1989
Chiarini, M., "La probabile identità del 'cavaliere di Malta' di Pitti," *Antichità viva* 28, no. 4 (1989), pp. 15-16.

Chiarini-Padovani 2003
La Galleria Palatina e gli Appartamenti Reali di Palazzo Pitti. Catalogo dei dipinti, eds. M. Chiarini and S. Padovani, 2 vols., Florence, 2003.

Christiansen 1986
Christiansen, K., "Caravaggio and 'l'esempio davanti del naturale,'" *Art Bulletin* 68 (1986), pp. 421-445.

Christiansen 1990
Christiansen, K., *A Caravaggio Rediscovered: The Lute Player*, exh. cat. (New York: Metropolitan Museum of Art), New York, 1990.

Christiansen–Mann 2001
Christiansen, K. and J.W. Mann, *Orazio and Artemisia Gentileschi*, exh. cat. (Rome, New York, Saint Louis), New York, 2001.

Cinotti 1983
    Cinotti, M., *Michelangelo Merisi detto il Caravaggio: Tutte le Opere*. Reprinted from *I Pittori Bergamaschi, Il Seicento*, vol. 1, Bergamo, 1983.
Cole 2005
    Cole, J., "Se di fuori è dorata, dentro è d'oro: Maffeo Barberini, Michelangelo il giovane e Galileo," *Belfagor*, Anno LX, no. 355, fasc. 1 (January 2005), pp. 1-26.
Cortis 2002
    Melitensium Amor: Festschrift in honour of Dun Gwann Azzopardi, eds. T. Cortis, T. Freller, and L. Bugeja, Malta, 2002.
Cropper 1991
    Cropper, E., "The Petrifying Art: Marino's Poetry and Caravaggio," *Metropolitan Museum Journal* 26 (1991), pp. 193-212.
Cutajar 1989
    Cutajar, D., "Caravaggio in Malta: His Works and His Influence," in Farrugia Randon 1989, pp. 1-18.
Cutajar 1999
    Cutajar, D., *History and Works of Art of St. John's Church, Valletta-Malta*, 3rd. ed., Malta, 1999.
Dal Pozzo 1703–1715
    Dal Pozzo, B., *Historia della Sacra Religione di Malta*, 2 vols.: I, Verona, 1703; II, Venice, 1715.
Degiorgio–Fiorentino 2004
    Degiorgio, S. and E. Fiorentino, *Antoine Favray (1706–1798): a French Artist in Rome, Malta, and Constantinople*, Malta, 2004.
Denaro 1967
    Denaro, V., *The Houses of Valletta*, Malta, 1967.
Denunzio 2005
    Denunzio, A.E., "New data and some hypotheses on Caravaggio's stays in Naples," in London 2005, pp. 48-60.
Fabbri 2005
    Fabbri, M.C., "Agli albori del collezionismo caravaggesco presso la corte medicea. Ipotesi e nuove considerazioni," in Carofano 2005, pp. LXI–LXXVII.
Farrugia Randon 1989
    Caravaggio in Malta, ed. P. Farrugia Randon, Malta, 1989 (rev. ed.; orig. publ. 1983).
Farrugia Randon 2004
    Farrugia Randon, P., *Caravaggio, Knight of Malta*, Malta, 2004.
Florence 1922
    Mostra della pittura italiana del Sei e Settecento, exh. cat. (Florence: Palazzo Pitti), Rome, 1922.
Florence 1996
    Gregori, M. and G. Bonsanti, *Caravaggio da Malta a Firenze*. exh. cat. (Florence: Palazzo Vecchio), Milan, 1996.
Florence 1999
    Gregori, M. and G. Bonsanti, *Caravaggio al Carmine: Il Restauro della "Decollazione del Battista" di Malta*, exh. cat. (Florence: Chiesa del Carmine), Milan, 1999.
Freedberg 1983
    Freedberg, S.J., *Circa 1600, A Revolution of Style in Italian Painting*, Cambridge (Mass.), 1983.
Freller 2002
    Freller, T., "On the trail of Caravaggio: Joachim von Sandrart in Malta," in Cortis 2002, pp. 289-300.
Friedlaender 1955
    Friedlaender, W., *Caravaggio Studies*, Princeton, 1955.

127

Galea 2002
   Galea, M., *Grandmaster Alophe de Wignacourt. 1601-1622*, Malta, 2002.
Gallo 2000
   Gallo, N., "Lo stemma dei Malaspina di Fosdinovo sulla tela del San Gerolamo del Caravaggio a Malta: Note e osservazioni," *Atti e Memorie della deputazione di storia patria per le antiche provincie modenesi* 22; Serie XI (2000), pp. 255-262.
Ganado 2001
   The Palace of the Grand Masters in Valletta, ed. A. Ganado, Malta, 2001.
Ganado 2003
   Ganado, A., *Valletta Città Nuova. A Map History (1566-1600)*, Malta, 2003.
Gash 1980
   Gash, J., *Caravaggio*, London, 1980.
Gash 1993
   Gash, J., "Painting and Sculpture in Early Modern Malta," in Mallia-Milanes 1993, pp. 509-603.
Gash 1997
   Gash, J., "The Identity of Caravaggio's 'Knight of Malta'," *The Burlington Magazine* 139 (March 1997), pp. 156–160.
Genius of Rome 2001
   Genius of Rome: 1592–1623, ed. B.L. Brown, exh. cat. (London: Royal Academy), London, 2001.
Giustiniani 1981
   Giustiniani, V., *Discorsi sulle arti e sui mestieri*, ed. A. Banti, Florence, 1981.
Gregori 1974
   Gregori, M., "A new Painting and some observations on Caravaggio's Journey to Malta," *The Burlington Magazine* 116 (October 1974), pp. 594-603.
Gregori 1991
   Michelangelo Merisi da Caravaggio: Come nascono i Capolavori, ed. M. Gregori, exh. cat. (Florence and Rome), Milan, 1991.
Gregori 1994
   Gregori, M., *Caravaggio*, ed. S. Zuffi, Milan, 1994.
Gregori 1996
   Come dipingeva il Caravaggio: Atti della giornata di studio, ed. M. Gregori, Milan, 1996.
Gregori 1997
   Michelangelo Merisi da Caravaggio e i suoi primi seguaci, ed. M. Gregori, exh. cat. (Thessaloniki), Florence, 1997.
Gregori 2000
   Gregori, M., "Due ritrattisti fiorentini da tenere in considerazione: Valore e Domenico Casini," *Gazette des Beaux-Arts* (February 2000), pp. 129-138.
Hess 1958
   Hess, J., "Caravaggio's Paintings in Malta: Some Notes," *Connoisseur* 142 (1958), pp. 142-147.
Hibbard 1983
   Hibbard, H., *Caravaggio*, New York, 1983.
ICR 1991
   Giralico, M.E. and M. Nimmo, et al., *Il San Gerolamo di Caravaggio a Malta: Dal furto al restauro*, Rome: Istituto Centrale per il Restauro, 1991.
Il Cinquecento Lombardo 2000
   Il Cinquecento Lombardo, da Leonardo a Caravaggio, ed. F. Caroli, exh. cat. (Milan: Palazzo Reale), Milan 2000.
Kitson 1967
   Kitson, M., *The Complete Paintings of Caravaggio*, New York, 1967.

Laking 1903
Laking, G.F., *A Catalogue of the Armour and Arms in the Armoury of the Knights of St. John of Jerusalem now in the Palace, Valetta, Malta*, London, 1903.

Langdon 1999
Langdon, H., *Caravaggio: A Life*, New York, 1999.

L'Idea del Bello 2000
L'Idea del Bello: Viaggio per Roma nel Seicento con Giovan Pietro Bellori, exh. cat. (Rome: Palazzo delle Esposizioni), 2 vols., Rome, 2000.

London 2005
Caravaggio, The Final Years, ed. N. Spinosa, exh. cat. (London: The National Gallery; shown earlier at Naples, Museo di Capodimonte), Naples, 2005.

Longhi 1992
Longhi, R., *Caravaggio* (orig. 1952 and 1968), ed. G. Previtali, Milan, 1992.

Macioce 1987
Macioce, S., "Caravaggio a Malta: il *S. Girolamo* e lo stemma Malaspina," in Calvesi 1987, pp. 175-181.

Macioce 1994
Macioce, S., "Caravaggio a Malta e i suoi referenti: notizie d'archivio," *Storia dell'arte* 81 (1994), pp. 207–28.

Macioce 1996
Michelangelo Merisi da Caravaggio: La vita e le opere attraverso i documenti. Atti del Convegno Internazionale di Studi, 1995, ed. S. Macioce, Rome, 1996.

Macioce 2001
Macioce, S., "Precisazioni sulla biografia del Caravaggio a Malta," in Palermo 2001, pp. 25-37.

Macioce 2002
Macioce, S., "Caravaggio a Malta: Precisazioni Documentarie," in Volpi 2002, pp. 155-169.

Macioce 2003
Macioce, S., *Michelangelo Merisi da Caravaggio: Fonti e Documenti, 1532–1724*, Rome, 2003.

Madrid–Bilbao 1999
Caravaggio, exh. cat. (Madrid–Bilbao), Milan, 1999.

Mahon 1947
Mahon, D., *Studies in Seicento Art and Theory*, London, 1947.

Maindron 1908
Maindron, M., "Le Portrait du Grand-Maitre Alof de Wignacourt au Musée du Louvre. Son Portrait et ses armes à l'Arsenal de Malte," *Revue de l'art ancien et moderne* 24 (1908), pp. 241-254; 339-352.

Mallia-Milanes 1993
Hospitaller Malta, 1530–1798: Studies on Early Modern Malta and the Order of St. John of Jerusalem, ed. V. Mallia-Milanes, Malta, 1993.

Malta 1999
Ciatti, M. et al., *The Return of Caravaggio's 'The Beheading of the Baptist' to Malta*, ed. T.M. Vella, Malta, 1999.

Marangoni 1922
Marangoni, M., *Il Caravaggio*, Florence, 1922.

Marini 1973-1974
Marini, M., *Michelangelo da Caravaggio*, 1st ed., Rome, 1973-1974.

Marini 2001
Marini, M., *Caravaggio "pictor praestantissimus." L'iter artistico completo di uno dei massimi rivoluzionari dell'arte di tutti i tempi*, 3rd ed., Rome, 2001.

Marini 2002
Marini, M., "Marino e Caravaggio: un ritratto nel contesto della Contarelli," in Volpi 2002, pp. 233-242

Marini 2003
Marini, M., Entry on Caravaggio's *Magdalene in Ecstasy*, in *Visioni ed Estasi: Capolavori dell'arte europea tra Seicento e Settecento*, ed. G. Morello, exh. cat. (Vatican), Rome, 2003, pp. 219-20.

Moir 1967
Moir, A., *The Italian Followers of Caravaggio*, 2 vols., Cambridge (Mass.), 1967

Moir 1989
Moir, A., *Caravaggio*, New York, 1989.

Mojana 1996
Mojana, M., *Orazio Fidani*, Milan, 1996.

Naples 2004
Caravaggio, l'ultimo tempo 1606–1610, ed. N. Spinosa, exh. cat. (Naples: Museo di Capodimonte), Naples, 2004.

Nicolson 1989
Nicolson, B., *Caravaggism in Europe*, ed. L. Vertova, 3 vols, Turin, 1989.

Orr 1982
Orr, L.F., "Classical Elements in the Paintings of Caravaggio," unpubl. Ph.D. dissertation, University of California, Santa Barbara, 1982.

Pacelli 1994
Pacelli, V., *L'ultimo Caravaggio, dalla Maddalena a mezza figura ai due san Giovanni (1606–1610)*, Todi, 1994.

Pacelli 1999
Pacelli, V., "Reconsideraciones sobre las vicissitudes artísticas y biográficas del ultimo Caravaggio,"in Madrid–Bilbao 1999, pp. 49-62.

Palermo 2001
Sulle orme di Caravaggio tra Roma e la Sicilia, eds. V. Abbate et al., exh. cat. (Palermo), Venice, 2001.

Pizzorusso 1983
Pizzorusso, C., "Un 'tranquillo dio': Giovanni da San Giovanni e Caravaggio," *Paragone*, no. 405, (November 1983), pp. 50-59.

Posèq 1987
Posèq, A.W.G., "A Note on Caravaggio's *Sleeping Amor*," *Source* 6, no. 4 (Summer 1987), pp. 27-31.

Posèq 1998
Posèq, A.W.G., *Caravaggio and the Antique*, London, 1998.

Posner 1971
Posner, D., "Caravaggio's Homo-Erotic Early Works," *Art Quarterly* 34 (1971), pp, 301-324.

Puglisi 1998
Puglisi, C., *Caravaggio*, London, 1998.

Rice 1997
Rice, L., *The Altars and Altarpieces of New St. Peters: Outfitting the Basilica, 1621–1666*, Cambridge, 1997.

Rossi 2000
Rossi, F., "Caravaggio e le armi. Immagine descrittiva, valore segnico e valenza simbolica," in Bergamo 2000, pp. 77-88.

Rubinstein 1986
Rubinstein, R., "Michelangelo's Lost *Sleeping Cupid* and Fetti's *Vertumnus and Pomona*," Journal of the Warburg and Courtauld Institutes 49 (1986), pp. 257-259.

Saccà 1907
Saccà, V., "Michelangelo da Caravaggio pittore. Studi e richerche," *Archivio Storico Messinese* VIII (1907), pp. 41-79.

Saints and Sinners 1999
Saints and Sinners: Caravaggio and the Baroque Image, ed. F. Mormando, exh. cat. (Boston College), Chestnut Hill (Mass.), 1999.

Sammut 1978
Sammut, E., "The Trial of Caravaggio," in Azzopardi 1978, pp. 21-27.

Schnapper 1994
Schnapper, A., *Curieux du Grand Siècle: Collections et collectionneurs dans la France du XVIIe siècle (II - oeuvres d'art)*. Paris, 1994.

Sciberras 1999
Sciberras, K., "Ciro Ferri's Reliquary for the Oratory of S. Giovanni Decollato in Malta," *The Burlington Magazine* 141 (July 1999), pp. 392-400.

Sciberras 2002[1]
Sciberras, K., "'Frater Michael Angelus in Tumultu': The Cause of Caravaggio's Imprisonment in Malta," *The Burlington Magazine* 144 (April 2002), pp. 229-232.

Sciberras 2002[2]
Sciberras, K., "Riflessioni su Malta al tempo del Caravaggio," *Paragone*, Anno LIII, terza serie, no. 44 (July 2002), pp. 3-20.

Sciberras 2004
Sciberras, K., "Da Napoli alla Valletta: ascesa e caduta di un cavaliere–pittore," in Sciberras–Stone 2004, pp. 61-66.

Sciberras 2005[1]
Sciberras, K., "From Naples to Valletta: the Rise and Fall of a Painter–Knight," in Sciberras-Stone 2005[1], pp. 61-66.

Sciberras 2005[2]
Sciberras, K., "'Due persone à lui ben viste': the identity of Caravaggio's companion as a Knight of Magistral Obedience," *The Burlington Magazine* 147 (January 2005), pp. 38-39.

Sciberras–Stone 2001
Sciberras, K., and D.M. Stone, "Saints and Heroes: Frescos by Filippo Paladini and Leonello Spada," in *The Palace of the Grand Masters in Valletta*, ed. A. Ganado, Malta, 2001, pp. 139-157.

Sciberras–Stone 2004
Sciberras, K., and D.M. Stone, "Caravaggio in bianco e nero: arte, cavalierato e l'ordine di Malta (1607–1608)," in Naples 2004, pp. 61-79.

Sciberras–Stone 2005[1]
Sciberras, K., and D.M. Stone, "Caravaggio in Black and White: Art, Knighthood, and the Order of Malta (1607–1608)," in London 2005, pp. 61-79.

Sciberras–Stone 2005[2]
Sciberras, K., and D.M. Stone, "Malaspina, Malta, and Caravaggio's *St. Jerome*," *Paragone*, Anno LXI, terza serie, no. 60 (March 2005), pp. 3-17.

Scicluna 1955
Scicluna, H.P., *The Church of St. John in Valletta*, Rome, 1955.

Sebregondi Fiorentini 1982
Sebregondi Fiorentini, L., "Francesco dell'Antella, Caravaggio, Paladini e altri," *Paragone* 383–385 (1982), pp. 107-122.

Sebregondi Fiorentini 1986
Sebregondi Fiorentini, L., "Francesco Buonarroti, cavaliere gerosolimitano e architetto dilettante," *Rivista d'Arte* 38, serie quarta, vol. II (1986), pp. 49-86.

Sebregondi 2005
Sebregondi, L., "Caravaggio e la Toscana," in Carofano 2005, pp. XLI–LIX.

Sebregondi *San Jacopo*
Sebregondi, L., *San Jacopo in Campo Corbolini a Firenze. Percorsi storici dai Templari all'Ordine di Malta all'era moderna*, Florence, 2005.

Sire 1994
Sire, H.J.A., *The Knights of Malta*, New Haven and London, 1994.

Sohm 2002
Sohm, P., "Caravaggio's Deaths," *Art Bulletin* 84, no. 3 (2002), pp. 449-468.

Spear 1971
Spear, R.E., *Caravaggio and his Followers*, exh. cat., Cleveland, New York, 1971 (2nd ed., 1975).
Spezzaferro 1974
Spezzarerro, L., "Detroit's 'Conversion of the Magdalene' (The Alzaga Caravaggio). 4. The Documentary Findings: Ottavio Costa as a Patron of Caravaggio," *The Burlington Magazine* 116 (October 1974), pp. 579-586.
Spezzaferro 2001
Spezzaferro, L., "La Cappella Cerasi e il Caravaggio," in M.G. Bernardini (ed.), *Caravaggio, Carracci, Maderno: La Cappella Cerasi in Santa Maria del Popolo a Roma*, Milan, 2001, pp. 9-34.
Spike 1978
Spike, J., "'The Church of St. John in Valletta 1578–1978' and the Earliest Record of Caravaggio in Malta: an Exhibition and its Catalogue," *The Burlington Magazine* 120 (September 1978), pp. 626–628.
Spike 2001
Spike, J.T., *Caravaggio*, New York and London, 2001 (with CD-rom catalogue).
Spiteri 2003
Spiteri, S.C., *Armoury of the Knights*, rev. ed., Malta, 2003.
Stone 1997[1]
Stone, D.M., "The Context of Caravaggio's 'Beheading of St. John' in Malta," *The Burlington Magazine* 139 (March 1997), pp. 161-170.
Stone 1997[2]
Stone, D.M., "In Praise of Caravaggio's *Sleeping Cupid*: New Documents for Francesco Dell'Antella in Malta and Florence," *Melita Historica* 12, no. 2 (1997), pp. 165-177.
Stone 2002
Stone, D.M., "*In Figura Diaboli*: Self and Myth in Caravaggio's *David and Goliath*," in *From Rome to Eternity: Catholicism and the Arts in Italy, ca. 1550–1650*, ed. P.M. Jones and T. Worcester, Leiden, 2002, pp. 19-42; revised version in *Caravaggio: Realism, Rebellion, Reception*, ed. G. Warwick, University of Delaware Press, forthcoming 2006.
Stone 2004[1]
Stone, D.M., "Caravaggio and Caravaggism', in *Europe, 1450-1789: Encyclopedia of the Early Modern World*, ed. J. Dewald, 6 vols., New York, 2004, I, pp. 382-388.
Stone 2004[2]
Stone, D.M., "Pitture del Merisi per la *Sacra Religione*," in Sciberras–Stone 2004, pp. 66-79.
Stone 2005
Stone, D.M., "Caravaggio's Paintings for the *Sacra Religione*" (rev. version of Stone 2004[2]), in Sciberras–Stone 2005[1], pp. 66-79.
Stone "Apelles"
Stone, D.M., "The Apelles of Malta: Caravaggio and his Grand Master," (forthcoming).
Stone–Sciberras
(see Sciberras–Stone)
Terrizzi, 1998
Terrizzi, F., "I Compagni Martiri di San Placido a Messina," in *L'Ordine di Malta ed il Tempio di San Giovanni Gerosolimitanto a Messina*, Messina, 1998, pp. 51-91.
Treffers 2000
Treffers, B., *Caravaggio: Nel sangue del battista*, Rome, 2000.
Vannugli 2000
Vannugli, A., "Enigmi Caravaggeschi: i quadri di Ottavio Costa," *Storia dell'arte* 99 (2000), pp. 55-83.

Venice 2000
   Lungo il tragitto crociato della vita, exh. cat. (Venice), Venice, 2000.
Vertot 1728
   Vertot, Abbé R.A. de, *The History of the Knights of Malta*, 2 vols., London, 1728.
Volpi 2002
   Caravaggio nel IV Centenario della Cappella Contarelli, Atti del Convegno, ed. C. Volpi,
   Città di Castello, 2002.
Zerafa 2004
   Zerafa, M.J., *Caravaggio Diaries*, Malta, 2004.

The Beheading of St John the Baptist, Valletta, Oratory of San Giovanni Decollato, detail

INDEX

Numbers in bold italics refer to figures and plates

Accarigi, Giulio, 40
Agucchi, Monsignor Giovanni Battista, 2
Anonymous painter,
    Portrait of Alof de Wignacourt in Armour (Verdala Palace), 70, 72, 99; ***22***
    Portrait of Alof de Wignacourt seated without armour (Rabat), 69, 74; ***24***
    Portrait of Alof de Wignacourt standing in Armour (Valletta, National Museum of Fine Arts), 73-75, 100; ***23***
    Portrait of Caravaggio (Mdina), 38; ***10***
Aratori, Lucia, 5

Baldinucci, Filippo, 81, 99, 101, 102
Barbary, 22, 73, 83
Barberini, Maffeo, 82, 127
Barberini family, 102
Barducci, Lionardo, 102
Bellori, Giovan Pietro, ii, 3-5, 14, 34, 38, 69, 70, 73, 74, 79, 89, 91, 93, 94, 97-99, 103-105, 109, 119, 125, 129
Benavente, Juan Alonso Pimentel Herrera, Conde de, 112
Benzo, Francesco, 40
Bernard, Pierre, 100
Bernini, Gianlorenzo,
    Ecstasy of St Theresa, 82
Bloemaert, Cornelis, 105
Borghese, Cardinal Scipione, 15, 119
Borghese family, 23

Bosio, Giacomo, 18, 30
Buonarroti, Francesco, 80, 82, 101, 102, 131
Buonarroti, Michelangelo, 2, 14, 82, 101, 102, 130
Buonarroti, Michelangelo the Younger, 80, 81, 83, 102, 127
Camarasa, Pietro Urrea, 104
Capeci, Giovanni Andrea, 21, 22
Capeci family, 38
Caracciolo, Battistello 84, 119, 124,
    Sleeping Cupid, 84, 102; ***29***
Caracciolo di San Vito, Niccolò, 87
Carafa family, 38
Caravaggio, Michelangelo Merisi da,
    paintings by or attributed to
    (* = rejected attributions):
    Adoration of the Shepherds, 12, 109, 115; ***7***
    Amore Vincitore, 14, 82
    Annunciation of the Virgin, 27, 95-98, 104, 109, 110, 114; ***33, XXII***
    Bacchino Malato, 6
    Bacchus, 7; ***2***
    Beheading of St John the Baptist, viii, 12, 14, 31, 38, 69, 84, 90, 92, 93, 95, 97, 99, 103, 104, 107, 108, 109, 113, 115, 123, 129, 132, 134; ***16, 32, 41, VIII-XVI***
    Boy with a Basket of Fruit, 6
    Burial of St Lucy, 12, 34, 108, 113, 115; ***17***
    Calling of St Matthew, 8, 9; ***3***
    Christ carrying the Cross with the Virgin and two Tormentors (lost), 116
    Concert of Youths, 6

Conversion of St Paul, 9; **5**
Conversion of the Magdalene, 25, 132
Crucifixion of St Andrew, 109, 110, 112
Crucifixion of St Peter, 9
David with the Head of Goliath (Rome), 103, 117, 119, 124, 132; **39**
David with the Head of Goliath (Vienna), 120
Denial of St Peter, 117
Ecce Homo*, 121
Ecstasy of St Francis (Hartford), 25
Flagellation of Christ (Naples), 112
Flagellation of Christ (Rouen), 123
Holy Family with St John the Baptist, 124
Inspiration of St Matthew, 9
Judith with the Head of Holofernes* (Naples), 122
Judith with the Head of Holofernes (Rome), 25
Lute Player, 6, 126
Madonna dei Palafrenieri, 10, 15
Madonna of Loreto, 10
Magdalene (Chapel of Italy, St John's), see Correggio, copy after
Magdalene* (Private Collection, Rome), 109, 110, 119, 129
Martyrdom of St Matthew, 8
Martyrdom of St Ursula, 117-119; **40**
Medusa, 1; **1**
Nativity with St Lawrence, 115, 120
Portrait of a Knight (Fra Antonio Martelli ?), 24, 85-89, 113, 128; **30**, *XX-XXI*
Portrait of a Man, 122
Portrait of Grand Master Alof de Wignacourt and a Page (Louvre), ix, 12, 70-79, 84, 86, 113, 114, 123, 129; **21**, *I-III*
Portrait of Grand Master Wignacourt "in aovato" (lost), 79
Raising of Lazarus, 87, 109, 113, 115; **36**
St Francis (Rome, S.M. della Concezione), 124
St Francis (Carpineto Romano), 124
St Francis (copy; Malta, private collection), 124
St Francis in Meditation (Cremona), 110
St Jerome Writing (Valletta, St John's), 24, 25, 69, 70, 84, 89-92, 96, 97, 99, 103, 107, 109, 113, 123, 124, 128, 129, 131; **31**, *IV-VII*
St. Jerome Writing (copy; private collection), 90, 103
St Jerome* (Worcester), 121
St John at the Spring* (private collection), 121
St John at the Spring* (Malta, private collection), 121
St John the Baptist (Munich), 120
St John the Baptist (Rome), 117, 118
Salome* (private collection), 121
Salome with the Head of St John the Baptist (London), 119; **38**
Salome with the Head of St John the Baptist (Madrid), 116, 119; **37**
Seven Works of Mercy, 10, 100, 110, 112, 113; **6**
Sleeping Cupid (Pitti), 14, 23, 24, 80-85, 101, 102, 114, 130, 132, **28**, *XVII-XIX*
Sleeping Cupid (copy; Indianapolis), 85, 102
Still Life with a Basket of Fruit, 3
Supper at Emmaus (London), 109, 110
Supper at Emmaus (Milan), 109, 110; **34**
Toothpuller, 120
Virgin and Child with Sts Dominic, Francis, Nicholas, and Vitus (Radolovich altarpiece; lost), 111
Virgin of the Rosary, 110, 111, 124
Carracci Academy, 3
Carracci, Annibale, 8, 9, 14, 132
   Assumption of the Virgin 9; **4**
Casini, Valore and Domenico, 128
   Portrait of Fra Francesco dell'Antella, 101
Cassar, Paolo, 28
Cassarino, 73
Catherine of Navarre, 39
Charles of Lorraine, Conte de Brie, 27, 39, 115
Charles II of Lorraine, 27
Charles V, Holy Roman Emperor and King of Spain, 17
Cigoli, Ludovico, 82
Clouwet, Albert, 105;
   Portrait of Caravaggio (engraving), **frontispiece**

Colonna, Costanza, Marchesa di
   Caravaggio, 5, 20, 119
Colonna, Marcantonio, 20
Colonna family, 10, 38
Coppini, Prospero, 32
Corbiaro, Leonetto, 28
Correggio (Antonio Allegri), copy after,
   Mary Magdalene (Chapel of Italy, St
   John's), 69, 89, 91, 103
Costa, Alessandro, 25, 91, 100
Costa, Antonio (or Antoniotto), 25, 91
Costa, Ottavio, 25, 91, 100, 132
Costa family, 23

d'Aleccio, Matteo Perez, 67
d'Alessandro family, 38
d'Arpino, Cavalier (Giuseppe Cesari),
   5, 6, 8
David, Jacques-Louis, 13
d'Este, Cesare, Duke of Modena, 112
de Franchis, Tommaso, 112
dell'Antella, Francesco, 18, 23, 24, 79,
   80-85, 101, 102, 131, 132,
   Map of Valletta, 101; 9
dell'Antella, Niccolò, 80, 101
del Monte, Cardinal Francesco Maria,
   6, 7
del Sera, Cosimo, 88, 103
de Ponte, Giovanni Pietro, 32, 37, 38, 40
di Giacomo, Nicolo, 115, 116
Domenichino (Domenico Zampieri), 3
Doria, Gian Andrea, 25
du Bus, Louis Perrin, 74, 100

Evelyn, John, 70, 99

Félibien, André, 2
Fidani, Orazio,
   Sleeping Cupid, 85, 130
Finson, Louis, 122
Florence, 22, 27, 80, 82, 84, 88, 132
Francis, Prince of Lorraine, 27

Galileo Galilei, 82, 127
Garagona, Bartolomeo, 104
Garzes, Grand Master Martino, 29
Gentileschi, Artemisia, 1, 84, 126,
   Sleeping Venus, 84
Gentileschi, Orazio, 1, 84, 99, 103, 126,
   Diana as Huntress, 99
   Executioner with the Head of St John the

Baptist, 103
Gigli, G.C., 1
Giorgione, 5, 67
Giotto, 94
Giovanni da San Giovanni, 84
   Tranquility (Sleeping Cupid), 84
Giustiniani, Cardinal Benedetto, 27, 39
Giustiniani, Marc'Aurelio, 27, 39
Giustiniani, Marchese Vincenzo, 3, 6,
   10, 14, 27, 39
Giustiniani family, 23,
Gonzaga, Margherita, 27, 39

Hals, Frans, 87
Henry II, Duke of Lorraine, 27, 39

Kilian, Wolfgang, 104,
   Criminal Tribunal in the Oratory, 18

Leonardo da Vinci, 5, 128
Leoni, Ottavio, 38,
   Portrait of Caravaggio, 38; 8
Lepanto, 19, 20, 73, 79
Liancourt, Duc de, 70, 99
Lomellini, Francesco, 30
Lotto, Lorenzo, 5
Louis XIV, 70

Malaspina, Ippolito, 23-27, 90, 91, 96,
   103, 128, 129, 131
Malvasia, Conte Carlo Cesare, 98
Mancini, Giulio, 98, 109
Marchese, Giacomo, 28, 39
Marino, Cavalier Giambattista, 1, 14,
   127, 129
Martelli, Antonio, 24, 25, 27, 36, 85-89,
   103, 113
Masaccio, 94
Mattei family, 23
Merisi, Fermo, 5
Messina, 12, 22, 25, 27, 28, 34, 36, 39, 40,
   85, 87, 88, 104, 108, 109, 115, 124, 132
Milan 2, 5, 13, 78, 79, 100
Minniti, Mario, 33
Moletti, Francesco, 36
Moretto da Brescia, 5
Murtola, Gaspare, 81, 85, 101

Naples 1, 2, 10, 12, 19-23, 25, 30, 39, 67,
   87, 90, 91, 98, 99, 104, 107, 110, 112,
   115-117, 119, 122, 124, 126, 127, 131

Osterhausen, Christian von, 37

Paladini, Filippo, 29, 67, 98, 131
Palermo, 12, 104, 115
Palestrina, 109
Paliano, 10, 109
Palma Vecchio, 5, 7
Palo, 13, 119
Paul V, Pope, 10, 15, 30, 38, 39, 92, 100
Pecci, Giovanni, 40
Peterzano, Simone, 5, 15
Picinino, Lucio, 100
Pinto de Fonseca, Grand Master
    Manuel, 100
Piscicello family, 38
Port' Ercole, 13, 120
Poussin, Nicolas, 2, 3
Preti, Mattia, 93, 103

Radolovich, Niccolò, 111, 112
Raphael, 2-4
Rembrandt, 1, 89
Reni, Guido, 1
Ribera, Jusepe,
    Penitent St Jerome (Cleveland), 99
Rodomonte Roero, Giovanni, 32, 40
Rome, 1, 2, 4, 5, 9, 10, 12, 14, 19, 20, 23,
    25, 30, 31, 81, 82, 89, 92, 93, 98, 102,
    103, 105, 107-109, 112, 119, 123-125,
    127-129, 132

Sandrart, Joachim von, 99, 127
Savoldo, Giovanni Girolamo, 5
Scannelli, Francesco, 98
Scaramuccia, Luigi, 98
Scaravello, Giovanni Battista, 40
Sersale family, 38
Sforza, Francesco, Marchese di
    Caravaggio, 5
Sforza Colonna, Fabrizio, 5, 20-23, 27,
    35, 39
Sforza Colonna family, 14
Sforza Colonna, Costanza (see Colonna,

Costanza)
Shakespeare, William, 4
Spacini, Geronimo, 100
Spada, Leonello, 73, 99, 100, 131
Spagnuolo, Roviale,
    Beheading of St John the Baptist, 93
Sustermans, Justus, 79, 101,
    Portrait of Fra Francesco dell'Antella, **27**
Syracuse, 12, 34, 104, 109, 115

Titian, 5
Tomassoni, Ranuccio, 10, 30, 107, 112,
    124
Torreglia, Orazio, 101

Urban VIII, Pope, 82, 127

Valette, Grand Master Jean de la, 18
Valletta, 12, 14, 18, 19, 22, 23, 25, 27, 31,
    32, 39, 67, 75, 82, 99, 101, 107, 127,
    128, 131, 132, 134
van Somer, Hendrick,
    Penitent St Jerome, 70, 99
Vasari, Giorgio,
    Beheading of St John the Baptist, 93
Velázquez, Diego, 1, 87
Verdalle, Grand Master Hughes de
    Loubens de, 38
Verdelain, Jean-Jacques de, 100
Villamena, Francesco,
    Map of Valletta (after Francesco
    dell'Antella), **9**
Vittoriosa (Birgu), 18

Wignacourt, Grand Master Alof de, 5,
    12, 19, 20, 22-25, 28-30, 34, 35, 38-40,
    69, 70, 72-74, 78-80, 84, 86, 87, 91, 97-
    100, 102, 103, 113, 114, 119, 122, 127
Wright of Derby, Joseph, 13

Zagarolo, 109
Zuccaro, Federico, 2